Improve Your Sailing IQ

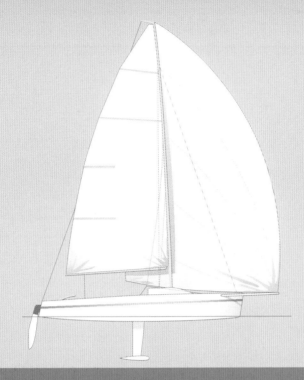

Improve Your Sailing IQ

John Driscoll

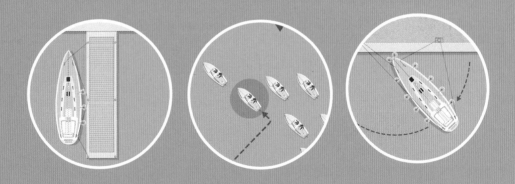

BARRON'S

A QUARTO BOOK

First edition for the United States,
its territories and dependencies
and Canada, published in 2003 by
Barron's Educational Series, Inc.

All inquiries should be addressed to:
Barron's Educational Series, Inc.
250 Wireless Boulevard
Hauppauge, New York 11788
http://www.barronseduc.com

Copyright © 2003 Quarto Inc.

International Standard Book No. 0–7641–2256–8

Library of Congress Catalog Card No. 2001099140

QUAR.IYS

Conceived, designed, and produced by
Quarto Publishing plc
The Old Brewery
6 Blundell Street
London N7 9BH

Project Editors: Tracie Lee Davis, Fiona Robertson
Designer and Art Editor: Elizabeth Healey
Editor: Sally MacEachern
Assistant Art Director: Penny Cobb
Photographer: Ian Howes
Illustrators: Patrick Mulrey, Andrew Green, Richard Burgess
Proofreader: Anne Plume
Indexer: Pamela Ellis

Art Director: Moira Clinch
Publisher: Piers Spence

Manufactured by:
Pica Digital Pte Ltd, Singapore
Printed in Singapore
by Star Standard Industries Pte Ltd
9 8 7 6 5 4 3 2 1

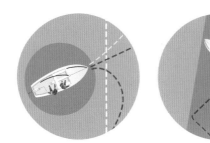

Contents

Introduction

The very fact that you're reading this

suggests that you're one of the millions of people worldwide who already enjoys the sport of sailing. You don't need to be convinced of its appeal—and the chances are that you're hooked for life! The sport is unique in its range and diversity, catering for enthusiasts of all ages, from young children competing in their tiny Optimist dinghies to dedicated professionals surfing around the world in the marathon ocean races.

It's hardly a new sport. Sailing vessels have been used for trading for thousands of years but it's generally acknowledged that sailing purely for pleasure originated in the Netherlands. The first recorded yacht race took place on the River Thames, England, in the late seventeenth century, and the world's first yacht club was established in Cork, Ireland, nearly three hundred years ago.

In "Racing Skills," you'll find out how to use good tactics to gain places at each turning mark in a race.

But competitive sailing is only one aspect of the sport. For every person who races regularly at club level, there are hundreds more whose enjoyment comes from using their skill at harnessing the natural power of wind and water to cross lakes, seas, and oceans. In the sport of cruising under sail, the challenge comes from making the most efficient use of boat and equipment in order to make the best progress.

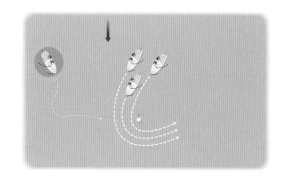

Why buy this book?

The bookshelves are full of "learn to sail" books on both sailing dinghies and cruising yachts. Some even claim to cover the whole sport in a single volume! The truth is that you never stop learning, even when you've been sailing for a lifetime.

This book is aimed at people who have already learned the basic skills and who are hungry to learn more. It assumes that you've sailed a conventional dinghy or small sailboat, but that you'd be keen to tackle a catamaran or performance boat if the opportunity presented itself when you were on vacation. Alternatively, you might be tempted by the idea of chartering a cruising yacht.

For many years I've enjoyed helping people to improve their sailing skills at all levels of the sport. In fact, during my years as Principal National Coach for the Royal Yachting Association, many people told me that I must have the best job in the world! The greatest challenge comes from encouraging people continually to stretch their ability.

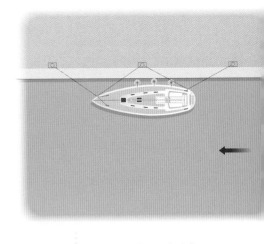

"Cruising Skills" is full of ideas on better boat handling under sail or power, including how to leave a quay in difficult conditions.

How to use this book

The book's question and answer format is designed to stretch your thinking muscles, test your knowledge, and encourage you to think about techniques and skills. To discover how much you really know, study the options for each question carefully before turning to the answers. In some cases, there'll be only one right answer. In others, more than one of the possible solutions may be correct, depending on various factors.

Sailing is an inclusive sport, which can be enjoyed by women and men of all ages and backgrounds. The text sometimes refers to the helmsman and crew as "he," but this is done for brevity rather than any other reason.

Finally, because sailing is such a wide-ranging sport, I feel we've only scratched the surface of some of the topics covered. I hope this taste will increase your thirst for knowledge and encourage you to seek out even more. Good sailing!

"The Boat and Equipment" will remind you of many basic principles, including how to avoid riding turns on winches.

John Driscoll

1 The Boat and Equipment

Take a stroll around any boat show, marina, or boat park, and you'll be faced with a huge variety of hull shapes, rigs, and deck gear. Although most boats have a great deal in common, it's important to recognize the differences that will affect your enjoyment of the sport.

Matching the boat and equipment to your sailing needs and skill level is a good first step. Knowing how to use that equipment to best advantage is even more important.

If you're an experienced sailor, use the questions in this section to discover how wide your knowledge is, and how much useful advice you'd be able to give to people coming into the sport.

1.1

Hull shapes and function

With literally hundreds of different classes available, how do you choose the right one for you? It's not simply a question of budget, as some racing sailboats may be worth more than a small cruising yacht. How much do you know?

Q1 A novice friend is anxious to get afloat as soon as possible and has asked for your advice on his final shortlist of four sailboats. The racing pedigree isn't important because he wants the boat for coastal day-sailing and picnics with his partner. He should choose:

A The 16-foot (4.8m), double-chine boat with aft mainsheet and spinnaker.

B The 14-foot (4.2m), double-chine boat with spinnaker.

C The 14-foot (4.2m), shallow, round-bilge boat with single, sleeved sail.

D The 15-foot (4.5m), round-bilge boat with single trapeze.

Q2 A catamaran enthusiast is trying to persuade you to convert from a monohull sailboat. **Which of her claims are true?**

A Catamarans are much faster than monohulls in light airs.

B Catamarans are much lighter than monohulls.

C Catamarans are much faster than the conventional monohulls in both moderate and fresh winds.

D Catamarans can sail faster than the wind speed.

Q3 As an experienced sailor in small, open dayboats, you're now planning to introduce your young family to sailing a cabin yacht. There's one for sale in the boatpark, with a tall rig set forward in the boat, a large cockpit, and a wide, flat hull with a deep fin keel. Which of the following characteristics would you expect from her?

A Slow to tack and jibe, due to the hull shape.

B Poor windward performance in light weather, due to the keel configuration.

C Difficult to sail upwind in strong winds, due to rig size and hull shape.

D Poor directional stability offwind, due to rudder size.

Q4 You've noticed that some cruising yachts have two keels angled slightly away from the vertical, rather than one on the centerline of the boat. This is:

A To distribute the ballast weight more evenly.

B To allow the boat to dry out easily.

C To reduce the draft, as compared to a single-keeler.

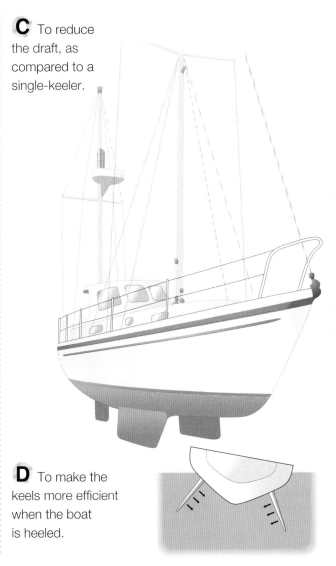

D To make the keels more efficient when the boat is heeled.

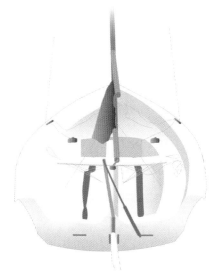

With so many classes on the market, it's vital to match the design to your sailing needs.

Answer: C D

The belief that catamarans are faster than monohulls is mostly true, but it's useful to understand why. The reasons have nothing to do with weight per se, as an 18-foot (6.4m) cat may weigh the same as an 18-foot (6.4m) monohull. Because the catamaran's weight is split between two thin hulls, the wave-making resistance is much lower, allowing the boat to go faster. This does not apply in very light airs, when it's the frictional resistance of the hulls that is critical. The other consideration is that the cat's stability and wide shroud base allow it to carry a powerful rig. When it comes to cruising boats, catamarans are lighter than monohulls because they don't need a lead or iron keel to keep them upright.

Multihull speed is due to powerful rigs and low wave-making resistance.

Answer: B

It's always dangerous to give advice when it's a matter of personal choice, but the principle here is to match the design to his purposes. The larger boat is obviously intended for day-cruising because the aft mainsheet leaves the cockpit clear. However, it will be heavier and more difficult to get on and off the beach than the others. The hull shape isn't really relevant these days, but deeper, hard-chine boats tend to be designed for general sailing rather than racing. The spinnaker will be great fun when your friend's confidence increases, whereas the single-sail boat leaves nothing for the crew to do.

Match your choice of boat to your sailing plans, and be realistic. Points to look for are:
A) rig size;
B) deck and cockpit layout;
C) hull shape;
D) keel configuration.

Answer: C

Many small sports cruisers are designed to give an exciting performance when sailed by a strong, competent crew, but they aren't necessarily the answer if you're looking for a boat to sail short-handed. The clues here are the size of rig and cockpit, which imply that the boat is designed to be raced by several people, whose weight will contribute to upwind stability. With a lighter crew, the boat is likely to be a flyer upwind in light weather, and the wide, flat underbody should make it stable offwind. However, it will be a handful in stronger wind conditions.

Answer: B C

Twin-keel yachts are popular in coastal areas with drying harbors. Although they do not perform as well to windward as a single-keeled yacht, they take the ground easily when the tide goes out. This makes them much more suitable for drying moorings. The fact that one keel might be vertical, and thus working efficiently when the boat is heeled, is offset by the fact that the other keel is creating additional drag. For many people, this loss of performance is acceptable as a penalty for the great practical advantage of drying out easily.

The slight loss of performance is compensated by low draft and the ease of drying out.

The Boat and Equipment

1.2

In the boatpark— small sailboats

The yacht chandlers are full of shiny, go-fast gear, but how much of it is really necessary? Concentrate on the essentials, or you may find yourself distracted from getting the best out of your boat.

Q5 You enjoy your sailing, but you often find that you come ashore wet and cold, whereas others seem to stay dry and comfortable. You are:

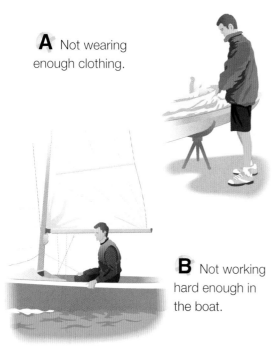

A Not wearing enough clothing.

B Not working hard enough in the boat.

C Not wearing the right kind of clothing.

Q6 You're planning to move into a different class of sailboat and notice that there is an adjustable ram built into the mast gate. The purpose of this is:

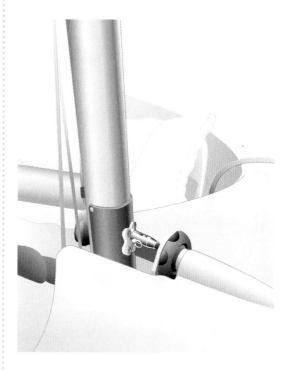

A To allow for masts of different section to be used in the mast gate.

B To allow the mast bend to be controlled in different weather conditions.

C To protect the mast against shock loading when sailing in waves.

Q7 You have seen that many of the trapeze rings on sailboats in the park have strops allowing for adjustment. This is to cater for:

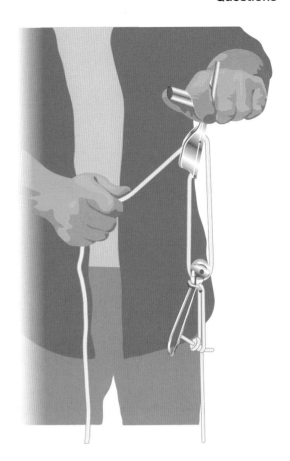

A Differences in height among crews.

B Whether the helmsman or the crew is using the trapeze.

C Whether you're sailing in medium or strong winds.

D Whether you're sailing in flat water or waves.

Q8 Attached to the bridle wire on your catamaran is a short wire with a colored streamer hanging from it. The main function of this is:

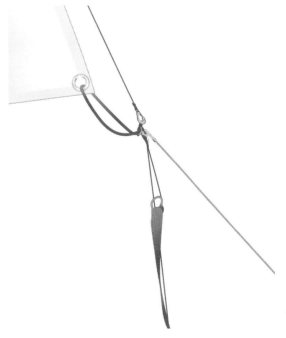

A To indicate which racing class you're in.

B To help you sail effectively upwind.

C To help you sail effectively downwind.

It's easy to stay warm, dry, and comfortable with the right clothes.

Answer: B

Mast rams like these are used on some of the most popular international classes. They limit the fore-and-aft movement of the mast at deck level, and hence its ability to bend when vang tension is applied. In moderate winds you'll sail with the ram wound tight, and ease it progressively as the wind increases.

Answer: C

It's important to choose clothing that suits the type of sailing you're doing. In high-performance dinghies you'll need a dry suit or wet suit to stay warm, but in a general-purpose dinghy or a cruiser you'll need waterproofs, preferably the breathable type. Wear lightweight layers underneath to give you ease of movement, preferably made of pile fabrics that wick the moisture away from your skin. Even in warm climates, it's important to wear a lightweight waterproof layer to keep the spray and salt off your skin.

Full power for moderate winds

Ram eased and vang tensioned in strong winds

A further tip is to ease the ram in very light winds to flatten the sail.

In marginal conditions you'll find a higher trapezing position much more comfortable.

A8 Answer: C

Although it's possible to sail a catamaran directly downwind, it's far more efficient to sail it on a series of reaches (see page 67). The bridle wind indicator is a common—and very simple—means of getting it right. If the streamer is at 90 degrees to the hulls, you're on the best course.

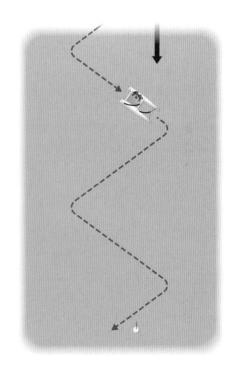

Tack downwind for best effect.

A7 Answer: C

Although the adjustment might possibly be used for any of the options given, the main purpose is to adjust your trapezing position according to weather conditions. In strong winds, you'll be out on the wire continually and the ideal position is to have the body as flat as possible to get the maximum righting effect from your weight.

In medium winds, however, you are likely to be moving in and out of the boat much more often and it's much less tiring to use a higher position. It also avoids the likelihood of you ending up in the water if you try to come in from the wire too quickly.

1.3

Deck gear and fittings
—cabin boats

The principles of sailing cabin boats are exactly the same as for small, open boats, but the size and power of the sails call for different equipment to handle them. In addition, the increased range of a larger boat calls for more gear. How much do you know about the important bits?

Q10 You've made the transition from small sailboats and have bought a one-off sports-cruising yacht. Each time you use the genoa sheet winches, you end up with a jam caused by riding turns. What's the cause?

A Your technique is wrong.

Q9 You're starting to race a small cabin sailboat on a lake. You notice that other boats in the park have compasses. However, there is no need for real navigation, so what's the point of having a compass?

A To help get you home in poor visibility.

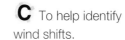

B To help establish which end of the start line to choose.

B The way the boat is set up is wrong.

C The genoa sheets are the wrong size for the winch.

C To help identify wind shifts.

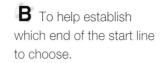

D The sheets are made of the wrong material.

Q11

Several of the yachts in your local marina are equipped with a wire that runs along each side deck. The wires look the same thickness as the shrouds, but are secured to deck-eyes near bow and stern. These are:

A Anchorage wires for a boom tent when in harbor.

D Attachment lines for your fend-offs.

B Jack lines for attaching safety harnesses when the crew are working on deck.

C Anchorage wires for alternative genoa-sheeting positions in very light winds.

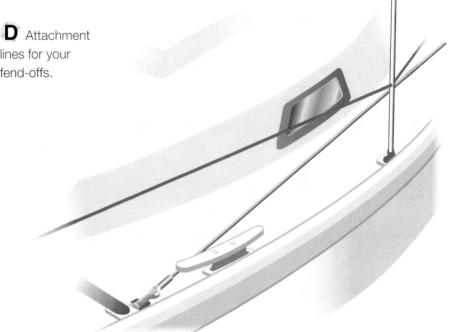

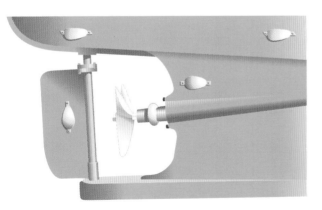

Q12

As you walk around the boatyard you notice that several cruising yachts have shiny, egg-shaped lumps of zinc bolted onto the outside of the hull. These are for:

A Protection against lightning strikes.

B Protection against galvanic action.

C Protection against osmosis.

D Protection against buildup of weed.

Answer: B C

Although it is possible to get away with not having a compass on a lake, it is useful for establishing the mean wind direction and whether there are any patterns to the wind shifts. In this way, you can identify shifts quickly and make the best advantage of them (see page 112). Because start lines are not always set at exactly 90 degrees to the wind, you can check start line bias by sailing along the line, noting the heading, and comparing it to the mean wind direction.

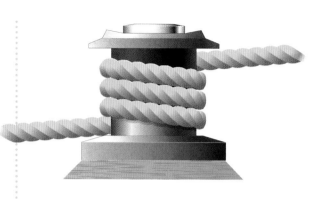

With deck-mounted equipment, mount your winches on teak pads to get the right angle for the sheet.

Answer: B

The cause of the problem is most likely to be the angle of the genoa sheet lead from the last turning block to the winch. If it causes the sheet to come in from above the horizontal, you are destined to have riding turns every time you use the winch. If the winch and turning block are both deck-mounted, just mount the sheet winches on pads. The winches should be high enough to cure the problem. Meanwhile, to clear a riding turn, simply take the load off the winch as follows. Tie a spare rope onto the sheet ahead of the winch (using a rolling hitch) then take this to another winch and tension it. You will then be able to free the wrap.

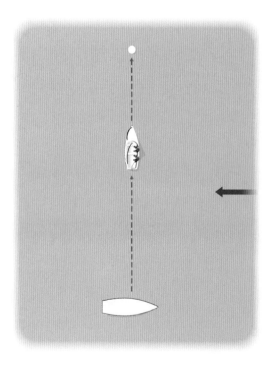

Sail along the line, noting the compass direction. If this is less than 90 degrees to the mean wind direction, you're sailing toward the favored end of the line.

A11 Answer: B

When you have to leave the cockpit to go forward in bad weather conditions at sea, it is much safer to clip your safety harness to a jack line that runs the length of the yacht, instead of moving the harness from one strong point to another. On some yachts, the jack line is of webbing, rather than wire, so that it lies flat and doesn't roll underfoot.

Keep a regular check on your anode and replace it when it starts to look like this.

Harness jack lines are vital to offshore safety. Use them!

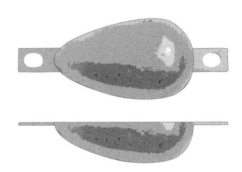

A12 Answer: B

Whenever different metals are in proximity in salt water, there's a possibility of galvanic action (sometimes called electrolysis), which can cause expensive corrosion. Even a fiberglass yacht needs a sacrificial anode to prevent damage to the propeller and skin fittings. This is one shiny gizmo in which you definitely need to invest.

Fundamentals

No matter how far you progress in the sport of sailing, a sound knowledge of the fundamentals is essential. Even at the Olympic level, medals have been won and lost when one sailor's attention wavered from the basic principles that govern how the boat and sails interact.

In new or difficult circumstances, or when the pressure's on because of competition or weather, it's useful to fall back on these fundamental principles. If you're an experienced sailor, you should be able to work through this section quite quickly. If any of the questions do slow you up, they're revealing important gaps in your knowledge.

2.1

Driving forces—**the five essentials**

Sail trim, boat trim, boat balance, course made good, and centerboard—master the five essentials in a small sailboat and you're well on the way to becoming an expert. When you alter one of the essentials, you'll have to consider all the others.

Q2

You're sailing on a reach with hull and sails well trimmed. Without using the rudder, how can you bear away?

Q1

When you try to bear away from a close-hauled course, the tiller feels heavy and the boat seems to slow down. You should:

A Ease the jib sheet off and lift the centerboard before you start to bear away.

B Ease the mainsheet as you pull the tiller toward you.

C Give the tiller a sharp tug to initiate the turn.

A Ease the mainsail and heel the boat to windward.

B Heel the boat to leeward.

C Sheet in the mainsail and heel the boat to windward.

D Ease the jib.

Q3 You've turned from a reach to sail closer to the wind, so you've sheeted the sail in. Although you're heading for a buoy, your boat seems to be slipping sideways through the water and you won't reach it. To avoid this, you should:

A Head up closer to the wind.

B Push the centerboard down.

C Heel the boat to windward.

Q4 In response to a strengthening wind, you've reefed the mainsail, but you now find that the boat is carrying excessive lee helm on the reaches, with a tendency to bear away all the time. You don't have a smaller jib to swap for the genoa, so what's your best solution?

A Take a few turns in the genoa around its luff wire.

B Lower the centerboard a little more.

C Let the genoa lift a little to spill wind.

D Sit out hard to keep the boat flat.

Always ease the mainsheet as you start to bear away. You should be aiming for a smooth, fluid movement.

 A2

Answer: A

Using the sails and hull to steer the boat is a really important fundamental skill. If you understand the effects of imbalance, you'll always sail efficiently. Boats are designed to be sailed upright; heeling creates an imbalance that causes the boat to turn. If the boat is heeled to windward, it will bear away from the wind (and vice versa).

The turning effect of the sails depends on the balance between jib and mainsail. To simplify the theory, think of the boat pivoting around a point just aft of the mast. By sheeting in the jib and easing the mainsail it will bear away (and vice versa).

Have the confidence to play around with boat balance and sail settings. Sheet in the jib to bear away (1) or the mainsail to luff up (2). By heeling the boat to windward, it will bear away without your having to use the rudder.

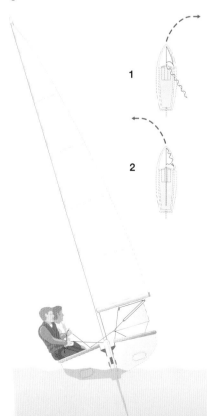

 A1

Answer: B

One of the most common errors made by beginners is their failure to match tiller movements with adjustments to the sheets. In this situation, the trimmed mainsail will help the boat turn toward the wind, not away from it, so it's essential to ease the mainsheet when bearing away. In extreme cases, failure to do this can cause a bent tiller or even a broken rudder blade!

Answer: **B**

In a small sailboat, every change of course should be accompanied by adjustments to the sheets and the centerboard. In this case, the increased leeway that comes from sailing close-hauled should be counteracted by pushing the centerboard down. Although it may be tempting to sail even closer to windward, this will simply slow the boat and increase leeway.

Start by lowering the centerboard. If this doesn't cure the problem, let the boat heel slightly to leeward.

Push the centerboard right down, but don't try to sail closer than close-hauled.

Answer: **B**

By reefing the mainsail and not the genoa, you have altered the whole balance of the rig. The quickest way to reduce the lee helm is to lower the centerboard a little from its normal reaching position. Alternatively, you could let the boat heel slightly to leeward, creating weather helm to offset the imbalance of the rig.

2.2

Getting afloat
and ashore

These are the times when you're most likely to have an audience, so it's important to think through each maneuver and have an escape route ready in order to avoid embarrassment, or worse.

Q5 Your catamaran is pulled up on a crowded beach with many others. There is a moderate wind blowing directly offshore. Having hoisted the sails, what's the best way to get off into clear water?

A Turn the boat downwind and jump aboard quickly.

B Get aboard yourself, have your crew walk the boat out into chest-deep water, and then bear away hard as your crew climbs aboard.

C With each of you sitting on one bow, let the boat drift downwind into clear water, and then climb aboard.

Q6 While you're out sailing, the wind has increased and is blowing directly onshore. The surf's up! What's the best technique for getting back to the beach?

A Luff up outside the shorebreak, drop the mainsail, and then run in under jib.

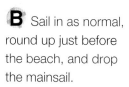

B Sail in as normal, round up just before the beach, and drop the mainsail.

C Lift the centerboard, prepare to lift the rudder, and go for it!

Q7 When you return to the jetty, and there is an onshore wind, your best approach is to:

Q8 As you head back to shore in your catamaran, you find that the offshore wind is gusty and variable in direction. What's the best landing strategy?

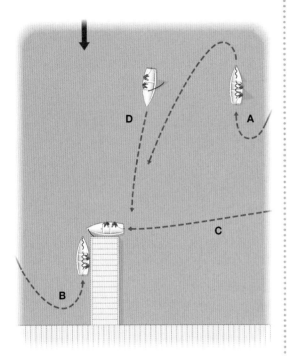

A Luff head to wind, drop the mainsail, and come in under jib alone.

C Approach on a reach, dropping the mainsail as you get within three boat lengths.

B Sail in past the jetty head, luff, and come alongside.

D Drop the jib when still some way to windward, and approach under mainsail alone.

A Roll up the jib and approach slowly under mainsail alone.

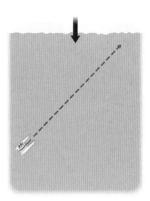

B Lift the leeward rudder and approach on the tack that gives the shallowest angle to the beach.

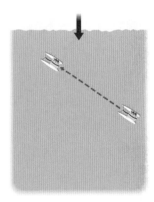

C Lift the windward rudder and free off the downhaul on the mainsail.

Answer: C

The other options are likely to end in embarrassment and damage. Nothing looks cooler than simply sitting on the bows while the boat drifts calmly out into safe water. Make sure that the mainsheet and traveler are freed right off before you leave. If you need a little extra steerage, use the jib!

Cool cat sailors find this the simplest way to leave a crowded beach.

Hold jib clew to fill sail and speed things up

Crew weight causes bow to act as skeg

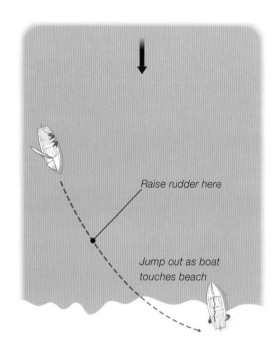

Raise rudder here

Jump out as boat touches beach

Large waves breaking on the beach leave no time for a hesitant approach.

Answer: C

Two principles are important here. The first is to spend the shortest possible time in the shorebreak, and the second is to keep the boat stern on to the waves as you approach. Any attempt to turn the boat close to the shore is likely to end in disaster, with a capsize and possibly a broken mast. This is no time for hesitation or half-hearted attempts. Approach fast on a very broad reach, raise the rudder at the last moment, and get out of the boat as it touches the beach. Once you have pulled the boat clear of the waves, turn it head to wind to lower the mainsail.

Answer: A

The most seamanlike option is always to approach slowly and under control. The only disadvantage is that you're committed, and will find it difficult to sail out again if things go wrong. Option B may look cool, but unless you are absolutely confident that there's enough water close inshore and that your mainsail will come down quickly and easily when needed, this maneuver could end in embarrassment, or damage.

Keep the power on and go for the bold approach.

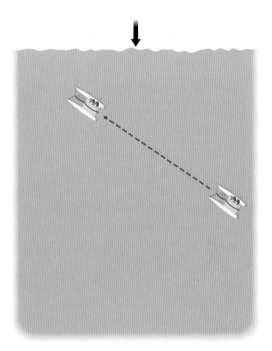

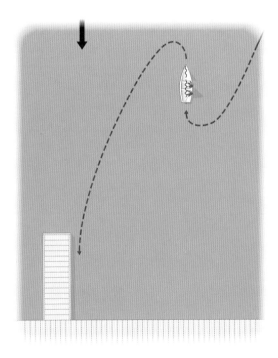

Stop to drop the mainsail far enough away from the jetty to get it tidied clear of the tiller, so that your approach isn't hindered.

Answer: B

In these conditions, the boat will stop very quickly when you ease the sheets, so it's essential to keep the power on until you're near enough for the crew to leave the boat. By raising the leeward rudder in advance, you'll have no need to go back to that side of the boat, and can concentrate on raising the windward rudder and sorting out the sails when you land.

Q9 Your dayboat is lying at a fore-and-aft mooring on an inland water, with others immediately ahead and astern. With a strong wind from astern, what's the best technique for getting away from the mooring?

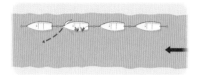

A Have the mainsail ready to hoist, raise the jib, sheet in, and give a sharp push on the tiller to clear the boat moored ahead.

B Let go the stern line, swing alongside the next boat down, and hoist both sails when head to wind.

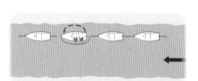

C Take a line from the bow of your boat to the stern mooring buoy, cast off from the buoy ahead, and turn the boat around before hoisting the mainsail and jib.

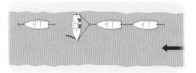

D Take bow and stern lines to the stern buoy. Adjust them until the boat is broadside to the wind, hoist the jib, and reach off into clear water before hoisting the mainsail.

Q10 You sail in a tidal area, and sometimes when you try to pick up a mooring you find that you can't stop the boat. You should:

A Take the mainsail down as you approach the mooring.

B Always make the final approach into the wind.

C Always make the final approach into the tide.

You've watched other club sailors on the lake approach their moorings and they always seem to judge the final swoop into the wind to perfection, stopping just as they reach the buoy. You can't match their style, so what should you do?

A Get the crew to pull the jib sheet in to windward as you make the final approach, in order to slow the boat more effectively.

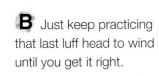

B Just keep practicing that last luff head to wind until you get it right.

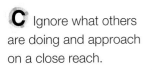

C Ignore what others are doing and approach on a close reach.

You've had a good afternoon's sail, but the wind is starting to die away as you return upriver to your mooring. The wind is behind you. What's your approach?

A Sail beyond the mooring, luff head to wind, and drift down onto the mooring with the current.

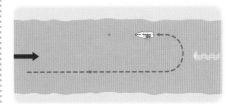

B Luff head to wind before you reach the mooring, drop the mainsail, and then run down toward the mooring under jib alone.

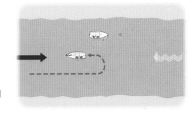

C Head straight for the buoy on the run, aiming to swing head to wind as you pick it up.

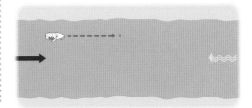

33

By swinging gently alongside the next boat, you'll be clear of the trot when you need to leave.

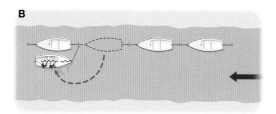

Answer: C

In a strong tidal stream, you should always make the final approach into the tide because that is the force acting on the boat when it stops. If the mainsail will be full on your final approach, take it down beforehand. However, if wind and tide are together, you'll need the mainsail for the approach. If the tide is slack, you should make your final approach on a close reach, easing the sheets as you near the mooring buoy, so that it is beside your weather shroud when you stop.

Answer: B C

The most elegant approach, assuming that you have adequate fenders to prevent any possible damage, is to swing alongside the next boat on the trot. You will not only be head to wind, but you'll have some clear space ahead of you when you're ready to set off. However, if you're in any doubt about causing damage, warp the boat around in your own mooring space until you can lie head to wind and hoist the sails.

The only exception to this rule is with a weak tidal stream against a strong wind. Look to see which way other boats are lying to judge your final approach.

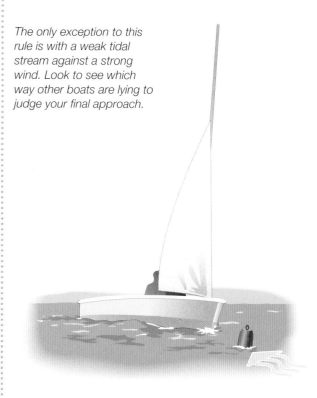

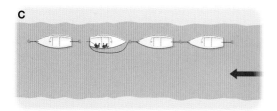

It will take longer to set up, but this is a safe alternative.

A11

Answer: C

Although it may seem that others are handling their boats well, there's no guarantee that they haven't just perfected some bad habits. The best way to approach a mooring is on a close reach, where you are able to control boat speed and direction very accurately. The danger with a "reach and luff" approach is that there's no room for error. Too slow, and you're left short of the mark; too fast, and the crew will have difficulty hanging on to the buoy.

By approaching on a close reach, you'll be able to control boat speed effectively.

Don't be afraid to stand for a better view of the buoy

Depending on wind strength, you can either let the jib flap or hoist a bit of mainsail to fine-tune your speed.

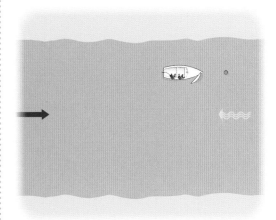

A12

Answer: B

Once you've lowered the mainsail and resumed your run under jib alone, you'll get a better idea of the comparative strengths of the wind and current. Assuming you've enough power in the jib to overcome the adverse current, all you have to do is ease the jib on the final approach to the mooring.

If the wind really is dying away, you might need to hoist the mainsail a short way up. You'll find there's a great deal of satisfaction in being able to control your speed minutely.

2.3

Rules of the road—**meeting other boats**

Although the international regulations for preventing collisions are logical enough, the skill lies in being able to interpret and apply them quickly and positively.

Q13

You're running by the lee, with the wind on the same side as your mainsail, when you see another sailboat crossing in front of you. But which tack are you on for give-way purposes?

A The wind is on your starboard side, so you're on starboard tack.

B Your boom is to starboard, so you're on port tack.

C As the wind is astern, you're not on a tack at all.

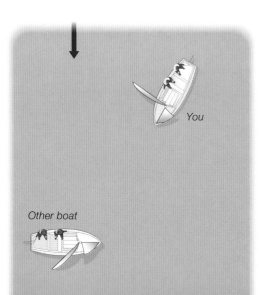

You

Other boat

Q14

You're reaching on port tack, about to overtake a slower sailboat that is heading in the same direction. Unfortunately, there's another sailboat heading toward both of you, on starboard tack. What should you do?

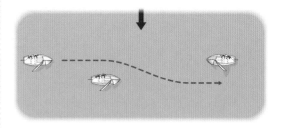

A Keep going until you're past the slowcoach and then bear away to leave the oncoming boat to port.

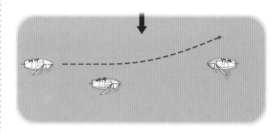

B As above, but luff harder to leave the oncoming boat to starboard.

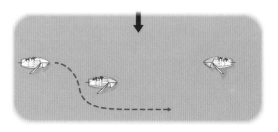

C Ease the mainsheet and bear away to pass to leeward of both boats.

Q15 You're sailing on a wide, slow-moving river. The banks on both sides are lined with bushes and trees. The wind makes your course a close reach, but which side should you choose?

A The center of the river for clear air.

B The windward side.

C The leeward side.

D The starboard side according to your direction of travel.

Q16 As you sail out of the estuary, you see that the foot-passenger ferry is about to set off from the shore on your port side. The best initial strategy is to:

A Keep going; after all, power gives way to sail.

B Do nothing yet, but keep an eye on the ferry to see how things develop.

C Head to port, so that you'll be able to pass safely behind the ferry when it crosses.

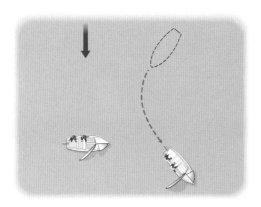

Either luff to pass ahead of the other boat (above) or jibe in good time and pass astern of her (below).

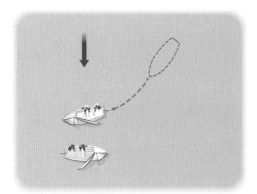

Answer: C

As overtaking boat, it's your responsibility to keep clear of the boat that you are passing. Equally you need to keep clear of the oncoming starboard-tacker. Frustrating though it may be, you need to drop to leeward and accept the momentary wind shadows of both boats. Next time, try to plan further ahead so the situation doesn't arise.

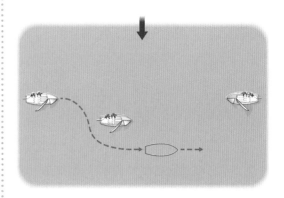

In crowded waters, always try to plan ahead, and avoid sudden changes of direction.

Answer: B

When the wind is directly astern, a boat's tack is determined by the position of the boom. The tack is the one opposite the boom. In this example, even though the boat is sailing "by the lee" you are still on port tack. As windward boat, you have to give way to the boat crossing ahead of you. Depending on your relative speeds and the distance between you, you could either luff slightly onto a fast broad reach and pass ahead of the other boat (avoiding the risk of an accidental jibe), or jibe in good time and pass astern of it.

A15

Answer: D

Given a fair wind, you should aim to sail on the starboard side of a river, or other channel, so that you will pass any oncoming boats port-to-port. If there are wind shadows close to the banks, it's perfectly reasonable to stay out far enough to remain in clear wind. The final consideration is the current. If you're sailing upriver it makes sense to keep out of the strongest current, which tends to flow in the center of the river, and the insides of any bends. Your course made good will take all these factors into account.

Your best course will be a compromise between getting clear wind, making best use of the current, and meeting other boats.

A16

Answer: B

Although the principle that power gives way to sail is true in open water, the rules change when boats are operating in restricted areas. In popular sailing areas, most ferry skippers will have some sympathy for the needs, speeds, and handling characteristics of sailboats and may wait for you to pass, but you shouldn't rely on this. Once the ferry has set off, don't be tempted to race across her bows; it's far safer to pass astern, but beware of wash or chains.

Once the ferry has set off, it's always safer to pass astern, rather than try to race across her bows.

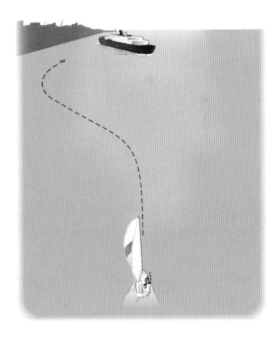

2.4 Capsize, man overboard, **and reefing**

Your repertoire of fundamental skills isn't complete until you can deal with stronger winds and common problems. In particular, your approach to a capsize will depend on the type of boat you are sailing.

Q17

Whoops! While out sailing in the estuary, you've capsized on the edge of the channel. The boat is inverted, and the tide is falling. Although you're 200 yards from the shore, the mast feels as if it's stuck in the mud. After three good attempts to get the boat upright, you feel like giving up. What should you do next?

A Keep going until you get the boat upright.

B Give up and swim for the shore.

C Dive under the boat and lower the mainsail.

D Give up and sit on the hull until you're rescued.

E Dive under the boat and undo the shrouds to release the mast. Right the boat and re-step the mast.

Q18

The catamaran you've rented off the beach has capsized, but the masthead float has stopped it from inverting. You're confident that you'll soon have it upright, but what next? What's the best way to get back on board?

A Over the side; just like your monohull.

B Over the main beam beside the mast.

C Over the aft beam in front of the tiller bar.

Q19 Your helmsman misses the toe straps after a tack, and suddenly you find yourself alone in the boat. Having regained control, what's the best way back?

Q20 When roller-reefing your mainsail, you find that the boom end tends to sag and keeps hitting you on the head when you tack. You should:

A Take fewer rolls in the sail.

C Buy a crash helmet.

B Take a tuck in the leech before you start the roll.

D Roll a waterproof jacket into the leech of the sail when you start.

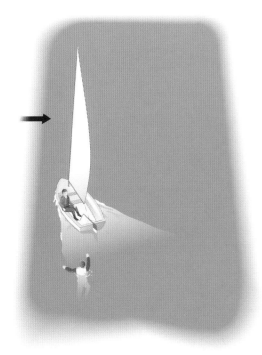

A Jibe around and then luff, stopping head to wind alongside him.

C Sail off on a broad reach, jibe, and then approach close-hauled.

B Sail off on a beam reach, luff and tack around, and then sail back on a reach, easing the mainsheet as you approach him.

D Sail off on a beam reach, tack around, and then sail downwind until you can approach on a close reach.

Answer: D

There will be times when you need outside assistance, and this is one of them! If you keep trying to right the boat, you're likely to end up without the strength to climb onto the hull, which is the safest place right now. Don't even think of swimming for the shore. It may look close, but the ebbing tide is likely to take you out to sea. By sitting on the hull, you'll stay much warmer than you would in the water, and you're a conspicuous target for rescuers.

Don't let go as you make your way to the aft beam.

It's safer to stop trying, and sit on the upturned boat to wait for help.

Answer: C

The biggest problem with a capsized cat is the amount of windage it offers. When it's capsized, it's likely to blow downwind faster than you can swim, so it's essential to hang on to part of it at all times. Similarly, when the boat is righted, it's likely to start sailing off, unless you have freed off the mainsheet and the traveler. If you try to climb in from position B, your legs will drift under the trampoline as the boat starts to move, and you'll find it difficult to get on board. From C, you're nicely fenced in between the aft beam and the tiller bar, so the boat can't escape!

Answer: D

It's always tempting to get back to the person as quickly as possible, but you must get control of the boat first. Tacking is safer than jibing, especially if the conditions are such that the helmsman was sitting out, using the toe straps. After tacking it is important to get back downwind, so that the final approach is on a close reach. This gives you the best opportunity to control your speed and course for the final approach, so that you stop with your helmsman alongside the windward shroud.

On a close reach, you can forget about the jib.

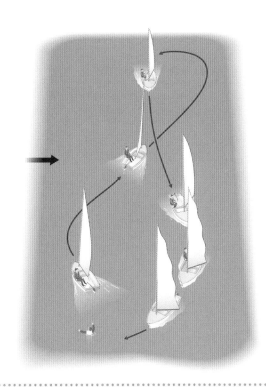

The end result will be a sail without creases and a level boom.

Answer: B

The triangular shape of the sail makes boom-end sag inevitable if you just try to roll the foot of the sail around the boom. Before you start, take a tuck in the leech and fold that around the boom, holding it in place with the extra turns as you roll the sail up. The exact amount varies according to the size of the sail, but you'll soon find out what's right for your boat. Partway through the reef, roll in a webbing strop or sail bag (leaving the cord hanging out) to give you somewhere to attach the vang.

Sailing Upwind

3

For hundreds—if not thousands—of years, ships and boats were barely able to make up ground to windward. Every coastline has the wrecks to prove it. But now even the simplest of children's sailboats can get upwind efficiently.

Nothing is given away easily, however, and each mistake or lack of finesse when sailing upwind will cost you dearly.

Although speed differentials within any one design class are very small when sailing upwind, the spread in any club fleet shows just how important your upwind sailing can be, both in the way you sail, and how you make the transitions from one tack to another. Apply the learning from this section, and you're guaranteed to get upwind more effectively.

Sail **trim**

3.1

As a beginner, you probably learned that to sail upwind you had to sheet the sails in tightly, and sail to windward on the edge of the "no-go" zone, about 45 degrees either side of the true wind direction. It's now time to discover how much more refined your windward sailing can be, whether you're sailing a small dayboat or a cruiser.

Q2

You've set the boat up with a full mainsail for Force 2 conditions, but once you're out at sea the wind drops away to almost nothing. You should:

A Increase fullness by easing the Cunningham and clew outhaul.

Q1

You're sailing close-hauled in 10 knots of wind with the jib sheeted fully in. You estimate that you'll reach your destination in about three or four more tacks. Meanwhile, the leeward telltales on the jib keep lifting. You should:

A Luff up.

C Ease the jib sheet.

B Bear away.

B Flatten the sail by tightening the Cunningham.

C Do nothing.

D Flatten the sail by tightening the vang and clew outhaul.

We're back to those telltales again! With three sets of telltales sewn into your genoa, you notice that the top windward telltales start to break before the lower ones. To get them all streaming at once on the beat, you should:

A Ease the genoa sheet a little.

B Move the genoa-sheet fairlead forward.

C Move the genoa-sheet fairlead aft.

D Rake the mast further aft.

E Tighten the vang.

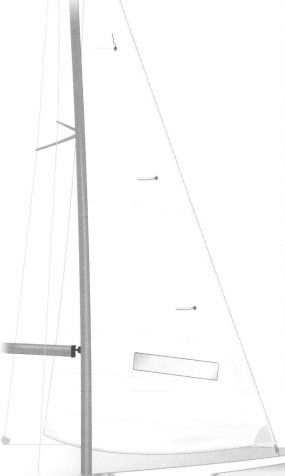

 You are sailing upwind in a strengthening wind and using the vang to control twist in the mainsail. As you increase vang tension, you reach the point where horizontal creases appear in the luff of the mainsail. To cure this, you should:

A Stiffen the mast at deck level with chocks or ram.

C Increase the Cunningham tension.

B Ease the Cunningham tension.

D Raise the centerboard a little.

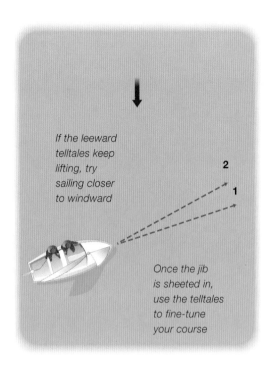

If the leeward telltales keep lifting, try sailing closer to windward

2

1

Once the jib is sheeted in, use the telltales to fine-tune your course

Answer: B

A2

In very light winds, it's vital to keep the air moving around the sails. If there's too much draft in the mainsail, the airflow is likely to stall. Although it goes against the principle of full sails for light winds and flatter sails in stronger conditions, the rule in very light winds is to flatten the sail. A little Cunningham tension will both flatten the sail and open the upper leech, but don't forget to ease it off again as soon as the wind fills it in.

Answer: A

A1

Even though the crew has sheeted the jib in fully, the telltales are showing that you're not sailing a true close-hauled course and that you can sail even higher to windward. Don't give away that extra distance—you've worked hard to get there. In this example you're sailing below your optimum course (1) so luff until telltales on both sides are streaming (2).

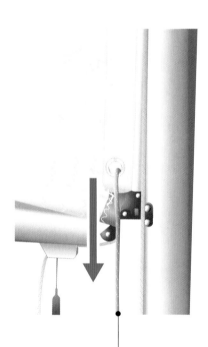

A quick tweak on the Cunningham will flatten the mainsail

If the top telltales break first, slide the fairlead forward; if the lower telltales break first, slide the fairlead aft.

A3 Answer: B

Your goal in establishing a jib-sheeting position is to create a uniform slot that matches the curve of the mainsail. The effect of wind shear means that the curves of both the mainsail and the genoa leeches will progressively open toward the head of the sail. The problem here is too much twist. Assuming that the genoa is sheeted in, slide the sheet fairlead forward until all the genoa telltales stream equally.

A4 Answer: A C

Your goal here is a flat mainsail with a tight leech. Increased vang tension causes the mast to bend. If the mainsail is not stiff enough, it will crease before you have sufficient leech tension. The increased Cunningham tension will remove the creases. It will also pull the position of maximum camber forward, counteracting the effect of the wind, which tends to push maximum camber aft.

Match your increased vang tension with Cunningham and mast ram to flatten the sail, but allow the upper leech to twist.

49

Tacking

3.2

Each time you make a transition from one tack to another, you're giving up speed and distance. Getting it right is not only satisfying, but can actually gain ground, especially in light weather.

Q5 You're starting to feel at home in your single-hander, but the boat still has a tendency to stop head to wind when you're tacking, especially in waves. How do you escape this? By:

A Pulling the tiller sharply toward you and pushing it slowly back to the centerline three times.

B Pushing the tiller away from you and keeping it there, while holding the boom out with the other hand.

C Sliding your weight as far back as possible to allow it to pivot around the rudder.

Q6 You know that your single-hander tacks quickly, but even though you cross the boat as soon as you can, you seem to be slower out of the tacks than others. You should:

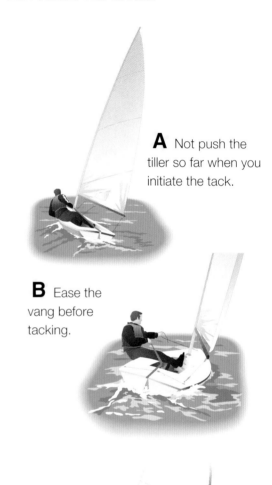

A Not push the tiller so far when you initiate the tack.

B Ease the vang before tacking.

C Wait longer before changing sides.

Q7 You've progressed from a general-purpose sailboat to a high-performance, twin-trapeze boat and want to make the most of tacking. You should:

A Plan everything beforehand, initiate the tack, and then come in together, standing throughout the tack.

B Leave the crew on the trapeze until the last minute, but come in early yourself from the wire, sit on the rack until the crew comes in off the wire, and then initiate the tack.

C Get your crew in off the trapeze early to sort things out properly before each tack.

Q8 When trying to roll-tack in light winds, you find that your boat fails to accelerate as much as others around you, even though they have the same crew weight. What's the cure?

A Bear away a little just before the tack.

B Roll the boat further as the bow comes head to wind.

C Ease the mainsheet during the first roll.

D Wait until the boat is sailing close-hauled on the new tack before pulling it upright.

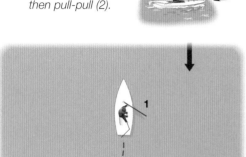

Stuck head to wind? Just remember to push-push (1), then pull-pull (2).

A5 Answer: B

The root causes of this common problem are usually a lack of speed into the tack, straightening the tiller before the tack is completed, or poor timing. Rather than waste effort and risk damage by trying to use the rudder as a paddle, let the wind do the work. If you push the tiller away from you and create some drive in the sail, the boat will move backward and turn onto your original course. When this happens, pull the tiller back to the centerline, sheet in the sail again, and you're away. Although you could pull the tiller toward you to initiate the turn, the boat would end up on the other tack with you on the leeward side!

A6 Answer: C

Ideally, you should wait until the boat starts to roll over on top of you before changing sides. This heels the boat to leeward and brings the mainsail into its new position, so it will fill quickly for the new tack. If you work on the basis that you should climb uphill to get to the new weather side, you've got the principle right. From outside the boat, it'll look nothing like as extreme as it feels to you!

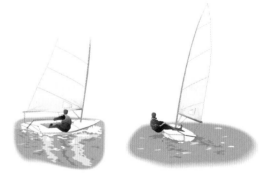

If it feels like you're climbing uphill to cross the boat, you've got it right.

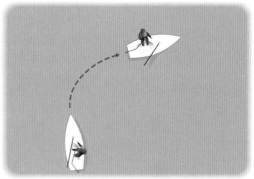

This technique will actually help you to pick up speed during light-weather tacks.

Answer: A

A7

Tacking twin-wire boats calls for confidence and determination. You must remember that when the boat is moving slowly there's a great deal of pressure on the rig. You cannot afford the "sit down and sort yourself out" approach or you'll be in the water. When the power comes out of the sails, stand up on the rack, unclip, move into the boat, ducking under the boom, and immediately go out onto the new windward side.

Powerful boats need positive handling.

Answer: A B

A8

By bearing away just before the tack, you'll help increase boat speed. The increased heel will create weather helm, helping the boat to turn into the wind. Exaggerate the roll to windward to the point where you think the boat is likely to capsize. Don't release the sheet until the boat is head to wind, and then ease it. When you're on the new course, you can pull the sheet in again to scoop more air past the rig. Change sides the moment the boat has turned halfway between head to wind and the new close-hauled course.

3.3

Variations in **waves and wind**

Sailors on ponds learn to deal with the vagaries of the wind. It's usually steadier out on the open sea, but there you'll find a whole new range of dynamics to affect the boat. How well can you master the techniques of sailing in waves and shifting winds?

Q10 With a pleasant Force 3 blowing and a sky full of white cumulus, you're enjoying a great sail on a very large lake. There's a regular pattern to the gusts and lulls, so what's your upwind strategy?

A Tack if a gust hits you when you're on port tack.

Q9 On the beat in a non-trapeze dayboat in strong winds, you should react to gusts by:

A Letting the boat heel to spill wind from the sails.

B Tack if a gust hits you when you're on starboard tack.

B Easing both the jib and mainsail.

C Easing the mainsail only.

C Ignore the gusts and lulls as the overall effect cancels out.

D Lifting the centerboard.

 It's a sizzling day, with plenty of white horses. You're crewing a trapeze boat upwind in big waves. To help your helmsman get through the waves at top speed, which of the following should you do?

A Move your weight forward as the boat rises to each crest.

B Move your weight aft just before each crest.

C Bend your knees when the boat levels out in the troughs.

D Hike out hard as the boat rises to each crest.

Q12 When you tack in waves, you find that the boat is apt to stop and that sometimes the bow is knocked off onto your original tack. You should:

A Start your tack when the boat is in the flat water at the bottom of the trough.

B Delay your tack until you find a flat patch of water.

C Initiate your tack when just past a wave crest.

A9 Answer: C

The priorities are to keep the boat level and moving quickly. Keep the crew weight out as far as possible, the jib sheeted in tight, and stay hard on the wind. Use the mainsheet to "feather" the mainsail in the gusts; excessive heeling will slow you dramatically and increase leeway. Raising the centerboard is a last resort for extreme conditions because it will affect your pointing ability.

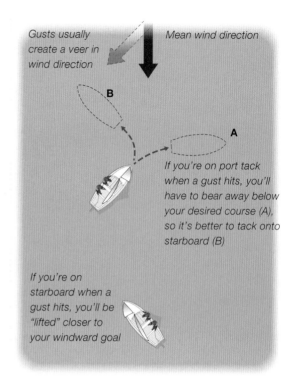

Gusts usually create a veer in wind direction

Mean wind direction

B

A

If you're on port tack when a gust hits, you'll have to bear away below your desired course (A), so it's better to tack onto starboard (B)

If you're on starboard when a gust hits, you'll be "lifted" closer to your windward goal

Keep the boat flat and the jib powered up all the time.

Allow the leading edge of the mainsail to lift (flap) slightly if necessary

A10 Answer: A

The keys here are the conditions and the location. The cumulus indicates unstable air, with vertical movement under the clouds. Away from the effects of wind bends caused by proximity to the shore, it's likely that the wind will veer in the gusts and back in the lulls. As the wind shifts could be 5 to 10 degrees, you'll gain considerably by using them. The rule is to tack on a gust if you're on port tack, and tack on a lull if you're on starboard.

Note: The opposite applies in the Southern Hemisphere—tack on a gust if you're on starboard.

A11 Answer: B C D

In these conditions, you should be adjusting your position continually according to your progress through the waves. As the boat climbs each wave, move your weight aft to reduce pitching and unstick the bow, ready to bear away after you've gone through the crest. Don't forget that going up the wave, boat speed will decrease and pressure on the sails will increase, so you'll need all the righting moment you can bring to bear. Down in the troughs, there's likely to be a drop in apparent wind strength, especially in the lower part of the rig, so be ready to bend your knees to keep the boat flat.

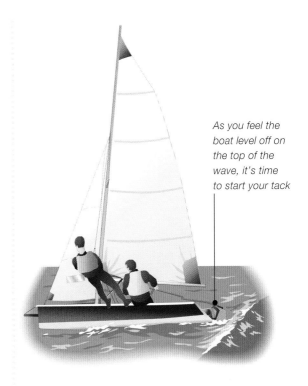

As you feel the boat level off on the top of the wave, it's time to start your tack

Aim for a smooth fluid movement in response to wind and waves.

A12 Answer: C

In these conditions, it's vital to hit each wave at speed and in full control. That means the tack must happen as the boat accelerates down the back of a wave. If you're sailing a trapeze-dinghy, it's even more important because of the extra time needed for the crew to come in off the wire. We all know that wave patterns are irregular, and that it's possible to find flat patches of water at times. However, if you waste time looking for them, you're likely to miss wind shifts and lose the concentration needed to take each oncoming wave properly.

4

Sailing Offwind and Downwind

What could be simpler than sailing offwind? Point the boat where you want to go, trim the sails until they stop flapping, and relax.

If that's your idea of offwind sailing, you're missing out on a world of techniques to improve your speed, comfort, and fun.

The speed differentials offwind are much greater than when sailing upwind; you can literally double your speed if you harness the power of the wind and waves effectively, whether in a monohull or multihull. And that's before you introduce the additional downwind sails that appear in the next section!

Use this section to test your knowledge of planing and surfing, as well as the art of jibing.

Reaching
techniques

4.1

It is easy to sail competently offwind, but it's here that the speed variation between average and well-sailed boats is most apparent, especially in moderate and strong winds. Are you a dawdler or a dragster?

Q1 **You're beam reaching in a small sailboat on a lake. As the wind dies away, you should:**

A Push the daggerboard down further than the normal position.

B Leave it in the same position.

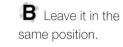

C Raise it slightly.

Q2 **Other boats plane for longer, whereas you tend to sink back into more sedate sailing. You should:**

A Luff slightly and sheet in as the wind eases.

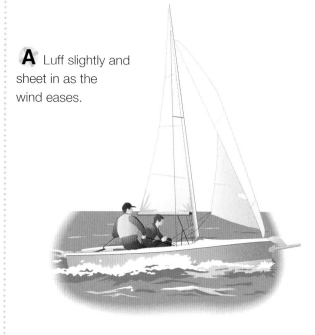

B Go on a strict diet and find a lighter crew.

C Ease the mainsheet as the wind goes aft.

Q3 In marginal planing conditions at sea, other boats of the same class are planing past you, but you can't seem to get the boat up onto the plane. Each time a gust hits, you heel and slow down, whereas others accelerate away. You should:

A Lower the centerboard and sheet in harder.

B Deliberately steer further offwind as you sail down the back of each wave.

C Sheet both mainsail and jib in rapidly, then ease the sheets again.

D Ease both mainsheet and jibsheet and raise the centerboard a little.

Q4 Conditions are on the limit, but you are determined not to give up! You've feathered the mainsail during the gusts, but you're overpowered on the reaches. Easing the mainsail just seems to make the boat go even faster! You should:

A Tighten the vang and move the jib fairleads forward.

B Ease the vang and move the jib fairleads forward.

C Ease the vang and move the jib fairleads aft.

D Tighten the clew outhaul and also the Cunningham.

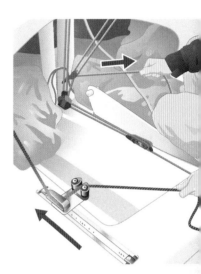

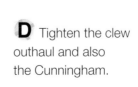

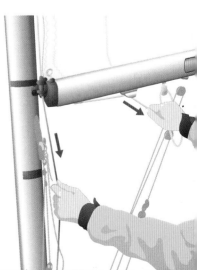

Answer: C

The key factor here is wetted surface area. There are two components to resistance—the wetted surface that the boat presents and the wave-making resistance. When the boat is moving slowly, there's little wave making, so your aim should be to reduce the wetted surface to a minimum by raising the daggerboard.

In doing this, you're likely to make more leeway, so be ready to sail above your proper course to compensate. This, in turn, will increase the apparent wind and hence boat speed. There's a fine balance here between getting it right and overdoing it, so go out and practice!

Remember that your boat speed affects apparent windspeed and direction.

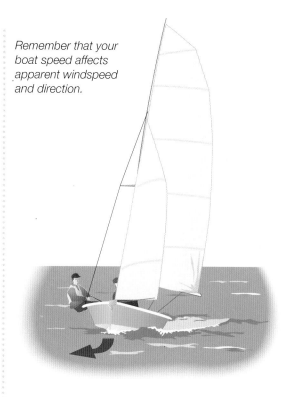

Lift the daggerboard to reduce wetted surface.

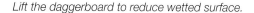

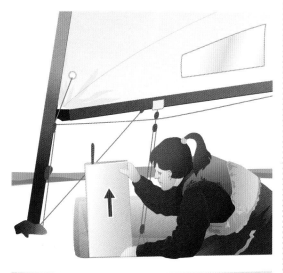

Answer: A

Remember that the boat's movement creates the apparent wind. When the wind increases and the boat accelerates, the apparent wind will move forward, and vice versa. As the wind eases, you can take advantage of the boat's momentum by luffing slightly and sheeting in to allow for the fact that the apparent wind has moved aft. This will allow you to maintain boat speed and so to stay on the plane for the longest possible time. With practice, you'll find there's a natural rhythm to your movements in these conditions, sheeting out to get the boat planing, and in again as the wind drops.

Answer: B D

To initiate planing, it's essential to keep the boat flat and use every extra ounce of power to unstick the hull. As a gust hits, bear away and ease the sheets to stop the apparent wind coming too far ahead. You don't need a lot of centerboard in these conditions—too much will create excessive heel and you'll never get up on the plane. Use the waves to initiate surfing, which, in turn, will increase the apparent wind and help get you planing.

Keep the boat flat to initiate planing.

Your goal is to have a flat mainsail low down, with the upper leech twisted so as to dump excess power.

Answer: C D

Until this point you have been increasing vang tension to gain maximum speed, but now it's time to dump power by allowing both mainsail and jib leeches to twist off. The vang is your control for mainsail twist. The jib-fairlead position will govern the shape of the jib leech. The extra tension in the outhaul and in the Cunningham will flatten the lower part of the mainsail, giving you power when you need it to keep going. Enjoy the conditions!

4.2

Downwind
techniques

Sailing directly downwind calls for different techniques from reaching, and you're always watching for the wind shift that could cause an accidental jibe.

Q6 When you're sailing dead downwind in your single-hander, you copy the fast guys and heel the boat to windward. Sometimes, however, you find that the boat starts to roll heavily one way and then the other, usually ending in a capsize. To avoid this, you should:

Q5 You're sailing downriver, downwind, on your desired course, when the jib suddenly goes "dead," fluttering limply behind the mainsail. You should:

A Do nothing—it's perfectly natural.

B Bear away slightly and sheet the jib out on the opposite side.

C Jibe the mainsail.

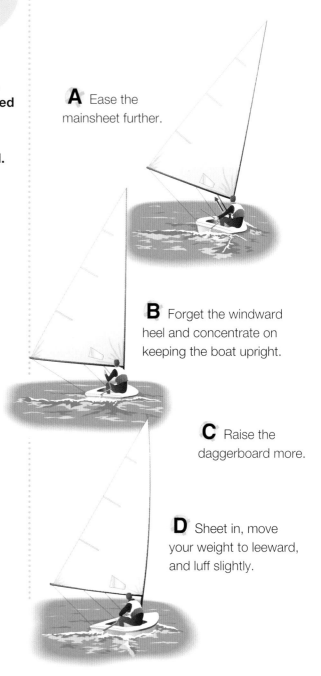

A Ease the mainsheet further.

B Forget the windward heel and concentrate on keeping the boat upright.

C Raise the daggerboard more.

D Sheet in, move your weight to leeward, and luff slightly.

Q7 You're running fast downwind in a moderate wind, but big waves. How can you achieve maximum speed?

 Q8 First time out in a beach catamaran, you find that it's great upwind, but a real drag sailing dead downwind. There's not even a spinnaker to make life interesting. What's the solution?

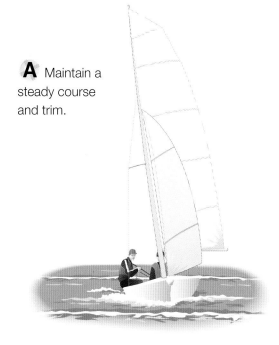

A Maintain a steady course and trim.

B Bear away in the troughs and luff on the crests.

C Luff in the lulls and bear away in the gusts.

D Luff in the troughs and bear away on each crest.

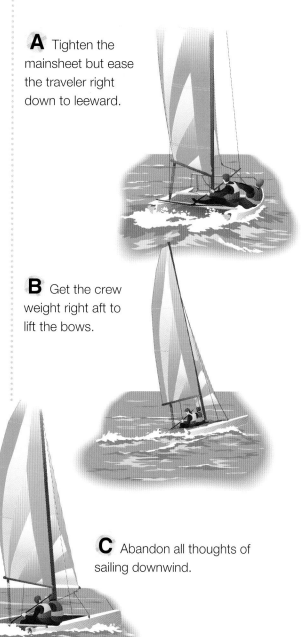

A Tighten the mainsheet but ease the traveler right down to leeward.

B Get the crew weight right aft to lift the bows.

C Abandon all thoughts of sailing downwind.

Answer: B

When the apparent wind is about 5 degrees away from a dead run, the jib will go dead. To sail the boat more efficiently, it's worth bearing away very slightly, so that you can set the jib on the opposite side to the mainsail. It's very quick to do, and the added speed will compensate for any slight extra distance you sail. On this heading, you'll need to watch out for variations in wind direction that might cause an accidental jibe.

In light and moderate conditions, the jib will need constant attention to keep it full.

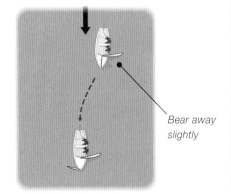

Bear away slightly

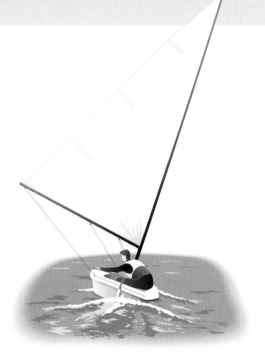

To stop the death roll, sheet in and hang on.

Answer: D

The technique of "kiting"—heeling the boat deliberately to windward—keeps the rig's center of pressure above the boat's center of buoyancy and thus reduces weather helm. Excessive kiting will make the boat unstable, leading to what's usually known as the "death roll." It's most common in strong winds, but can happen in moderate conditions. If it's just a gentle roll, you might stabilize the boat by lowering the daggerboard and sailing slightly more level. With a more violent roll, the only answer is to sheet in and grab the leeward rail with your tiller hand. At least you will be holding onto something and can pull yourself back into the boat.

Answer: C D

Wind and waves may be very different forces, but in this case the effects are the same. It's important to be square onto each wave as the stern lifts, so that you surf down its face without any tendency to broach. As you progress down the wave, luff slightly to ride it for longer and bring the apparent wind forward as you slow. Similarly, luffing onto a very broad reach will increase your boat speed, so that you are ready to make the best advantage of the next wave.

Answer: C

As a rule, catamarans should not be sailed dead downwind but in a series of reaches to maximize the apparent wind. The optimum angle relative to the true wind will in fact vary according to the design of the cat and the strength of the wind. As boat speed increases, the apparent wind moves further forward. So a catamaran should be sailed so that the angle of the apparent wind to the boat is never greater than 90 degrees.

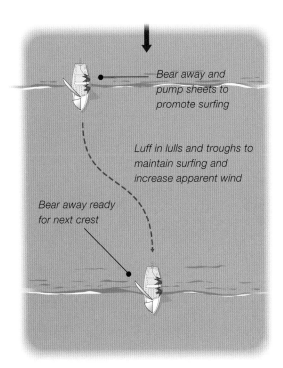

Bear away and pump sheets to promote surfing

Luff in lulls and troughs to maintain surfing and increase apparent wind

Bear away ready for next crest

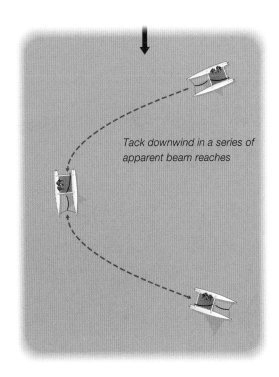

Tack downwind in a series of apparent beam reaches

Jibing

4.3

Making the transition from one jibe to another should be a simple maneuver, but there are various techniques to ensure that you get it right. How many do you know?

Q9 You have lost confidence when jibing your small sailboat because you often lose control after the jibe. The boat tends to spin around and sometimes capsizes. How can you maintain more control?

A Sheet the mainsail in before the jibe.

B Turn the boat through a larger arc, so the mainsail flaps after the jibe.

C Concentrate on keeping the boat heading downwind after the jibe.

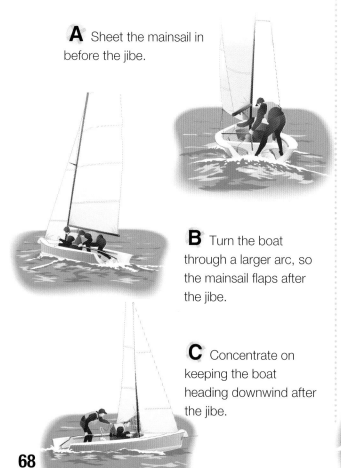

Q10 In moderate and strong winds, you find that the boat tends to luff violently after each jibe. What's the problem?

A Too little daggerboard or centerboard.

B Too much daggerboard or centerboard.

C Sails not trimmed in far enough.

D Moving too quickly across the boat.

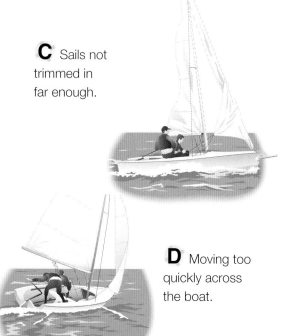

When you jibe a small sailboat in a strong wind, you should:

Sticking with the strong-wind jibe, but thinking about the waves, when's the best moment to start your jibe?

A Sit forward, so that the boat spins quickly around the centerboard.

B Slow down to regain control and then jibe the mainsail carefully.

C Plane down the waves at top speed and just go for it!

A At the bottom of the trough.

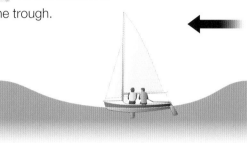

B Going down the face of a wave.

C Going up the back of a wave.

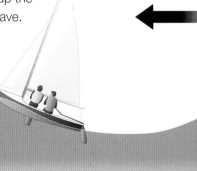

4.3 Jibing

Answer: C

A9 As the boom swings across in the jibe, center the tiller to ensure that the boat is heading directly downwind when the pressure comes onto the mainsail again. At the same time, you should already be moving across the boat so that in the middle of the jibe you, the tiller, and the boom are all positioned in the center of the boat.

Remember: Boom, tiller, and you should all be together.

Avoid the harsh pivot effect by raising the daggerboard or centerboard.

Answer: B

A10 If the daggerboard or centerboard is left too far down, it acts as a very effective pivot, making the boat spin quickly around. As long as there's enough board to give some grip on the water, it doesn't matter if the boat skids sideways as you jibe. On boats with low booms, you must ensure that the daggerboard isn't raised so high that it obstructs the boom in the jibe—that's a certain recipe for a ducking!

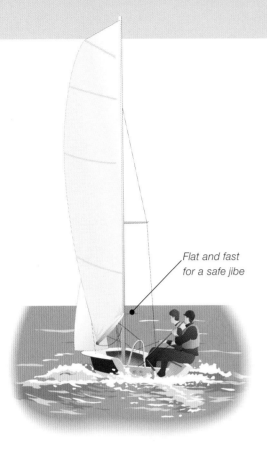

Flat and fast for a safe jibe

Answer: B

A12

This reinforces the principle of question 11, but brings in an extra consideration. By starting your jibe as you surf down the face of a wave, you'll not only be jibing at top speed, but you'll complete the jibe when you reach the comparative lull in the trough. That gives you time to regain full control and then plan your course for the next wave. In these conditions, you must be very positive about all your movements and cross the boat quickly to counter the effect when the mainsail starts driving on the new side.

Answer: C

A11

The ideal time to jibe is when the boat is moving quickly. This minimizes wind pressure on the sails. Hesitation is likely to lead to capsizing. It's also important to keep the boat flat when you go into the jibe. Any leeward heel will create weather helm, which will be working against the rudder movement as you try to bear away. Get this wrong and you could break the rudder blade!

You're at top speed, heading for the trough

THE NATIONAL
WATERSPORTS CENTRE
CANOLFAN CENEDLAETHOL

PLAS MEN

Advanced Skills

5

If you're happy with a two-sail boat, you might want to skip this section. Otherwise you risk developing an urge to experiment with lightweight sails and hiking aids, which can create a sizzling performance in the right conditions.

Many sailors shy away from the apparent complexity of spinnakers and asymmetrics, but the principles of handling them are almost as straightforward as the basic sails. It's just that things can get lively if you get the techniques wrong.

This section covers both conventional spinnakers and asymmetrics, together with trapezes and racks. If that sounds like torture, watch out!

5.1

Spinnaker
handling

There are many who say that downwind sailing is no fun without a spinnaker; yet this sail tends to cause difficulties for those who don't understand the principles behind its use. How much do you know about spinnaker handling?

Q2 You're sailing downwind in a light wind, with waves and a large swell left over from an earlier breeze. The best option for the spinnaker pole height and sheeting position is to:

Q1 You know the principle of keeping the spinnaker pole at right angles to the apparent wind, but how high should the outer end of the pole be set?

A Keep the pole height raised slightly above the normal position and ease the sheet slightly to keep the spinnaker full.

A So that the pole is horizontal from the mast.

B So that the pole is angled upward at 12 degrees.

C So that the two clews are level when the sail is set.

D So that the luff breaks first in the top third.

B Set the pole height to keep the clews level and trim the sheet normally.

C Drop the pole height slightly and overtrim the sheet.

Q3

You've mastered the basics of spinnaker handling in light winds but have problems when the wind increases. When you are power-reaching, you find that the boat heels excessively in the gusts, sometimes to the point of broaching. You should:

A Watch for each gust and bear away as it hits.

B Ease the mainsheet and be ready to bear away when the boat starts to heel.

C Watch for each gust, ease the spinnaker sheet gently as it hits, and then sheet in again.

 Q4

You are three-sail reaching at sea. The wind is an onshore Force 4 and the waves are giving you plenty of opportunities for exciting surfing. Your sailboat doesn't have roller furling for the jib, so you need to leave it up. You should:

A Sheet the jib in tightly and forget it while you concentrate on the spinnaker sheet.

B Set the jib for the reach and retrim as often as you can, cleating the spinnaker sheet momentarily.

C Ease the jib sheet until the front half of the sail is lifting and give all your attention to the spinnaker.

Answer: A C

In most conditions, your primary aim is to get the two clews at the same height. If your boat has a height adjustment for the inboard end of the pole (sliding track or different rings on the mast), you should choose the one that allows you to keep the pole closest to the horizontal. This will project the tack of the spinnaker the greatest distance ahead of the jib, and into clear air.

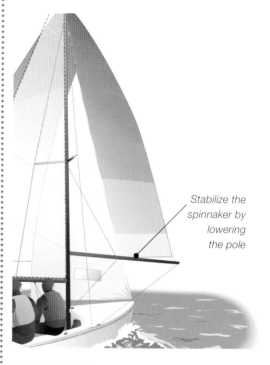

Stabilize the spinnaker by lowering the pole

Adjust inboard end if possible

Lift pole to get clews level

First get the clews level, and if you can adjust the inboard end of the pole, then aim to get the pole horizontal.

Answer: C

In most other conditions, you'd aim to keep the clews level, with the spinnaker luff curving equally along its whole length. The problem with this is that the shape—and hence the drive—of the sail will be affected by the up-and-down movement of the boat through the heavy wave slop. Lowering the spinnaker pole will make the sail more stable in these lumpy conditions.

Beware overeasing the sheet, as this could induce a heavy roll, which will slow the boat down even further. If the boat starts to roll, trim the sheet in, and then ease again as soon as you dare.

Answer: C

In these conditions, it's essential to be proactive. Your goal is to keep the boat as flat as possible with the spinnaker driving. One of you should watch to windward to anticipate the gusts and warn the other. As each gust hits, first ease the sheet, then sheet in harder as the boat accelerates and the apparent wind goes forward. In stronger conditions, you may also need to dump the mainsheet in the gusts in order to keep the boat flat.

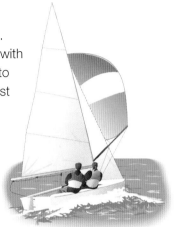

Aim for steady, not jerky movements. Ease as the gust hits, then sheet in as the boat accelerates.

In these conditions, don't worry if the jib isn't driving, but don't oversheet it.

Answer: C

Until you can find a crew with three hands, it's really best to forget about the jib in these conditions. The waves are moving across your desired course, so you should bear away on each one to promote surfing, and then luff again to stay on the wave for as long as possible. Trimming the spinnaker will demand all the crew's attention. You've got plenty of power with the mainsail and spinnaker, and the last thing you want is an overtrimmed jib disturbing the airflow over the mainsail and affecting the boat's balance. Helmsman and crew should concentrate on staying as close together as possible to help the motion through the waves, moving aft as the boat surfs down a wave and keeping the boat flat and level. Easing the vang is the most effective way of dumping wind out of the mainsail if you're overpowered.

Q5 You're shy-reaching under spinnaker, with the pole just clear of the forestay. On this heading, the spinnaker luff keeps curling back and the sail's in danger of flogging. You're reluctant to bear away below your desired course. You should:

Q6 You find that the spinnaker usually collapses during the jibe, whereas others keep their kite full throughout the maneuver. To cure this, you should:

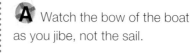

A Watch the bow of the boat as you jibe, not the sail.

A Ease the spinnaker guy and hold your course.

B Always round up to a reach after the jibe, to establish a good airflow over the spinnaker.

B Bear away very slightly.

C Lower the spinnaker.

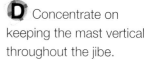

C Practice the maneuver.

D Concentrate on keeping the mast vertical throughout the jibe.

You've enjoyed an adrenalin-filled power reach, but the wind has increased and it's now time to drop the spinnaker. It is better to:

A Maintain the shy reach, lower the kite, and then unroll the genoa.

B As above, but unroll the genoa before lowering the kite.

C Bear away onto a run before lowering the spinnaker.

It's been an agonizing light-wind spinnaker reach against the tide, but you're finally approaching the leeward mark. The problem is that you're on starboard tack and you need to round the mark to port. The best strategy for the drop is:

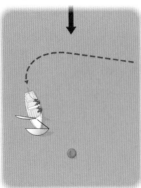

A To sail high, jibe onto port, and run into the mark, dropping the spinnaker to leeward just before you approach.

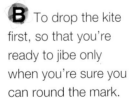 **B** To drop the kite first, so that you're ready to jibe only when you're sure you can round the mark.

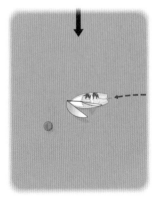

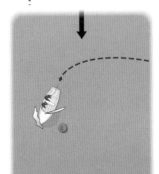

C To start the drop immediately before you jibe slowly to round the mark.

79

*Be ready to bear
away in order
to keep the
spinnaker driving
and the pole clear
of the forestay.*

*Ease main
slightly*

Answer: C D

Jibing a small sailboat with a spinnaker calls for efficient coordination between helmsman and crew. In a two-person boat, the helmsman usually looks after the spinnaker sheet and guy (with the tiller between his knees), while the crew sorts out the pole. This means that the helmsman can match the tiller movement to the position of the spinnaker. If you have difficulty keeping the spinnaker full, try to imagine the boat rotating under the spinnaker. By concentrating on the mast position, you'll keep the spinnaker stable and find that it stays set throughout the maneuver. Try it!

*Aim to rotate the
boat under the
spinnaker, keeping
the mast vertical.*

Answer: B

Accept that you'll have to sail a little below your desired course and make the most of any variations in wind direction to gain lost ground. In a planing boat, it's better to travel quickly (besides being much more fun) and then head up again after you've dropped the spinnaker. If you ease the guy until the pole touches the forestay, you start to create more drag than drive, because the tightly trimmed leach of the spinnaker will hook air back into the mainsail. It also puts strains on the rig and risks breaking the spinnaker pole. Drop the spinnaker in time to head comfortably for your destination under mainsail and jib.

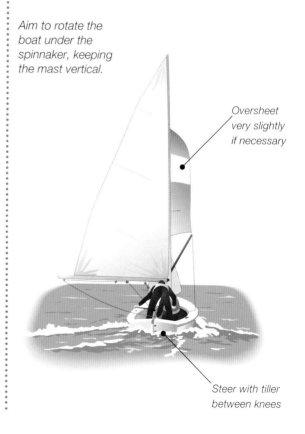

*Oversheet
very slightly
if necessary*

*Steer with tiller
between knees*

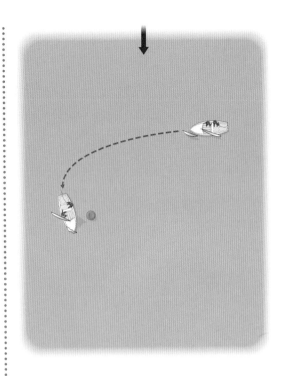

Answer: C

Unless you're racing and need to maintain your course right up until the mark, you can avoid all the hassles by bearing away first. The apparent wind drops, the mainsail shelters the spinnaker, and it all becomes so easy. In a small sailboat, the crew will need to stand by the mast to gather the spinnaker into its bag. In a cabin boat, you're more likely to bring the spinnaker down under the main boom.

If you can't bear away onto a run, unroll the genoa and leave it flapping to shelter the spinnaker.

Crew first removes pole, then gathers spinnaker

Answer: C

This technique is known as a float drop and, properly done, is one of the most impressive pieces of crew work you can demonstrate. It's most useful in conditions like those here, when it's vital to keep the spinnaker flying as long as possible to maintain downwind boat speed. Prepare by removing the pole and stowing it. Start as if you're going for a weather drop. As the helmsman bears away for the jibe, the crew releases the sheet and gathers the spinnaker on the weather side. When the mainsail crosses the boat, the spinnaker lies quietly behind it, and can be pulled down quickly while the helmsman trims the mainsail for the new course.

Trapezing

5.2

First seen as a means of allowing the crew of a two-person sailboat to gain extra leverage, the trapeze has spread to all kinds of sailboat, from single-handers to nine-person skiffs. Because the trapeze is so effective, smaller movements of body weight have a great deal of effect. Are you wired for speed?

Q10

You enjoy sailing a fast twin-trapeze catamaran, but find that your crew has difficulty staying in the right place, and doesn't respond to the wind and waves as you'd like. Worst of all, the boat tends to cartwheel in strong winds. You should:

Q9

You find it hard to get out onto the trapeze, and you are swinging forward all the time. To overcome this, you should:

A Use both hands on the trapeze handle.

B Put your back foot onto the gunwale first, and then use it to push yourself out.

C Put your front foot onto the gunwale first, and then use it to push yourself out.

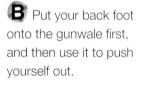

A Find a new crew who will use the toe loops

B Communicate more about what you're doing.

C Hand over the mainsheet.

D Hand over the traveler.

Asymmetrics

5.3

The modern asymmetric spinnaker (called a gennaker by some sail lofts) has transformed a whole section of sailing. With s roots somewhere between the Australian skiffs and ruising chutes, the asymmetric is ideal for lightweight oats that can sail faster than the wind. However, arge sails need positive handling. Can you cope?

It's your first outing in a sailboat with a short, fixed bowsprit and a large asymmetric. The wind's stronger than you might have hoped, but you are full of enthusiasm for the day. In these conditions, you should rig the asymmetric sheets:

You're ready to bear away and hoist the asymmetric. The way your boat is set up, the crew has all the ropes to hand, and so what should you do first?

A Outside the forestay, but inside the end of the sprit.

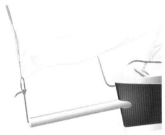

A Hoist the halyard, and then pull out the pole and tack.

B Launch the pole, pull the tack out, and then hoist the halyard.

B Outside everything, including the sprit.

C Pull out both halyard and tack together.

Ease jib to prevent cartwheel

Answer: C

In all boats there is a tendency for the crew to be pulled forward, simply because the trapeze wire is attached to the mast. The best technique for getting out easily is to hook yourself on and then swing out, pushing with your front foot and bending the knee of the back leg. To come in again, simply bend both knees and lift the back foot off the gunwale first, to avoid swinging forward into the shroud.

In all high performance boats, it's essential to communicate what you're planning to do.

Remember: Front Foot First!

Answer: B

Good communication is vital. Although the crew should be looking ahead to anticipate the waves, he's not psychic when it comes to knowing what you're about to do with the mainsheet or traveler. It may help if the crew uses his front hand for both the jib sheet and the handle when going out on the trapeze. This leaves his back hand for balance. He should also use the toe loops when out on the trapeze—after all, they're not there for decoration. Finally, the crew is in the best place to spot an imminent cartwheel. As the leeward bow starts to bury, whether because of excessive drive or an unhelpful wave, he can ease the jib sheet to reduce pressure and stabilize the situation.

Answer: B

Before you do anything, the crew should set the vang and jib sheet for the reach while the helmsman bears off downwind and balances the boat. Now get the pole and tack out. (On some boats, the tack line can be preset so that the tack is launched as the pole is run out.) Finally, hoist the halyard as quickly as possible, both to prevent the sail from falling into the water and to ensure that the sail is up before it fills. It's useful to mark the halyard at the point where it should emerge from the cleat. This gives you a reference point, so that you don't have to fight for the last yard of halyard once the asymmetric has filled. When you're confident about your hoisting, it's also useful to mark the sheets, so that they can be preset in the cleat with a couple of yards of slack. That way, when the sail is up, the crew can pick up the sheet and trim in the slack as she heads for the wire.

Set mainsail for reach

Mark your sheets and halyards with reference points for quick and efficient hoisting.

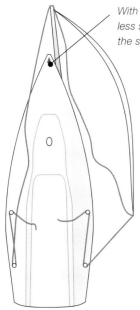

With more experience, and in less strong winds, you can rig the sheets inside

Answer: B

Until you're confident that you can handle an "inside" jibe, there's absolutely nothing wrong with the safe "outside" method. It may leave you feeling like you're on a stop-start city bus each time you jibe, but there's little chance of a wrap, or of the boat being knocked down in a gust. Some experienced sailors use the outside jibe in strong winds, especially in classes where there's not much room to get the gennaker around between the forestay and the gennaker luff. To avoid the risk of the lazy sheet dropping under the bow, tape an old sail batten to the end of the sprit.

This technique is most often seen in keelboat classes with short sprits.

Q13 On some boats, the sprit can be adjusted laterally. This is to:

A Enable the end to be set to leeward for clear air over the asymmetric.

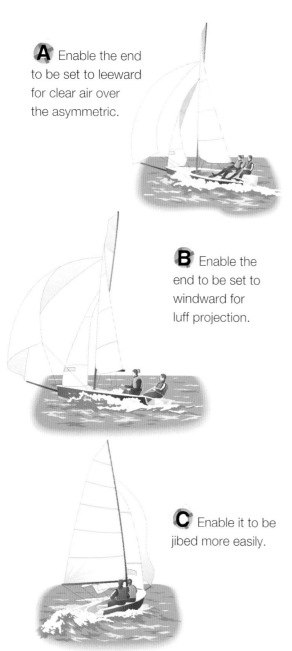

B Enable the end to be set to windward for luff projection.

C Enable it to be jibed more easily.

Q14 You are approaching a mark with the asymmetric full. You have to jibe around the mark to be on the right course. The correct order to jibe the sails is:

A Mainsail, gennaker, jib.

B Gennaker, mainsail, jib.

C Jib, mainsail, gennaker.

D Jib, gennaker, mainsail.

It's best to go into the jibe at full speed.

 **You're experiencing lee helm with your big asymmetric kite. You should:**

 **You're power-reaching to perfection. With the asymmetric full, you're screaming up toward a group of slower sailboats, ready to blast past them with huge grins on your faces. You should pass them:**

A Deliberately sail with the boat heeled slightly to leeward.

B Sheet the mainsail in harder.

C Ease the boom vang.

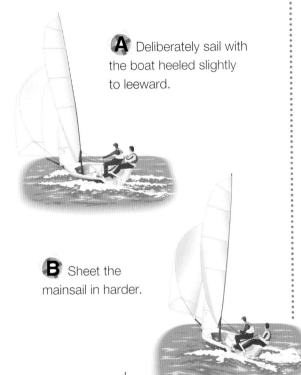

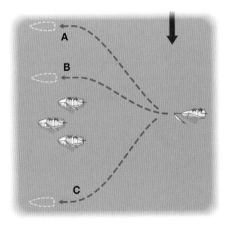

A Upwind, but five boat lengths to windward of them.

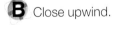 **B** Close upwind.

C Downwind, at least five boat lengths to leeward.

87

Answer: B

When you are close- or beam-reaching with an asymmetric, the pole end is normally set in line with the boat. If you have to sail further offwind, it pays to get the maximum luff projection, either by easing the tack line, or by tweaking the sprit to windward. Classes vary, but each class of boat will have a range of optimum downwind sailing angles, depending on wind speed and sail shape. If you can't get these from the class association, or the sailmaker, you'll just have to develop your own.

Initiate the jibe smoothly but positively, waiting for the gennaker clew to float forward before the stern goes through the wind.

Leave the jib until last

Set the sprit to windward

If you are sailing downwind, reset the sprit before each jibe.

Know your optimum downwind angle

Answer: A

The basic principle with asymmetrics is to hoist and jibe them like conventional spinnakers, but trim them like jibs. The hassle-free way to jibe with a big asymmetric is to jibe the mainsail first, then the gennaker, keeping boat speed as high as possible throughout. That way, you'll have a clear airflow over the gennaker. This will help float it all the way around the forestay, so you can sheet it in on the new side. The crew should maintain some tension on the old gennaker sheet while she pulls the new sheet across. This will prevent the upper leech blowing forward and creating a wrap. The helmsman should delay the turn of the boat so that he doesn't go stern to wind until the gennaker clew is past the forestay. Leave the jib lightly sheeted until both large sails are set, and then deal with it.

Answer: A

Because asymmetric kites are usually set on a bowsprit—and are very large in relation to the rest of the sail area—they have a tendency to unbalance the rig. Counter this by ensuring that the mainsail is developing full power and by allowing the boat to heel 10–15 degrees. The weather helm from the hull then balances the lee helm of the rig. Resist the temptation to oversheet the mainsail; it will cause the mainsail to stall and make things worse.

Don't oversheet the mainsail

Allow the boat to heel slightly, but don't overdo it, or you'll kill speed and cause a broach.

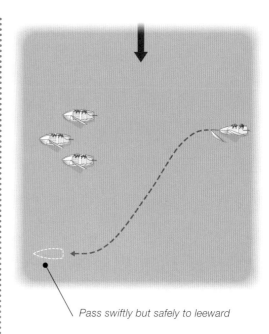

Pass swiftly but safely to leeward

The wind shadow may slow you momentarily, but that gives you time to wave and smile!

Answer: C

It's tempting to share your excitement with others, but there are a few factors to consider. As overtaking boat, you are legally the "give-way" vessel, and they won't think much of you stealing their wind as you blast past. Even more important is the fact that, if a gust hits as you're passing them, you are likely to bear away under the power of the asymmetric, whereas the slower boats are more likely to luff. I don't have to spell out the consequences of that!

Cruising Skills

6

There are some sailors for whom the appeal of small, open sailboats never dies. For most of us, however, the sheer freedom of being able to voyage under sail is a massive attraction. You are self-contained, self-sufficient, and propelled by natural energy resources. No wonder cruising appeals to those who want a contrast to today's busy lifestyles.

Your speed may never be greater than a bicycle's, you may have to shelter from the weather, or anchor to wait out a foul tide, but you can explore parts of your own country and others that are out of the reach of most people.

This ability to explore, while overcoming the natural challenge of the sea, is at the heart of cruising under sail. Test your knowledge to discover how ready you are to face the challenge of a larger boat.

Boat **handling**

6.1

As the principles of sailing a cruising yacht are identical to those of handling a small sailboat, most dinghy sailors make the transition to larger boats very easily. However, the size and weight of the boat, rig, and gear do call for changes in technique.

Q1 You've recently progressed from dinghy sailing to cruising and enjoy the comfort and extra equipment. You've noticed, however, that the boat tends to fall away to leeward after each tack, before picking up speed again. You should:

A Try tacking more quickly.

B Try tacking more slowly.

C Ease off the mainsheet as you luff for the tack.

Q2 It's a glorious sailing day and you're reaching at hull speed in your performance cruiser, under full mainsail and heavy No. 1 genoa, heading straight for your destination a couple of miles (3 or 4km) ahead. As the wind increases, you consider your strategy for reducing sail. You should:

A Put the first slab in the mainsail before changing down to a No. 2 genoa.

B Keep the mainsail driving and change the genoa for a No. 2.

C Increase the vang and backstay tensions.

Q3

You're sailing shorthanded and chose to heave to in order to reef. Now the reef's tidy and it's time to get going again. You should:

A Let the weather genoa sheet fly, and then sheet in the leeward sheet.

B Ease the weather sheet slowly while taking in the new one.

C Bear away, jibe, and then concentrate on where you want to go.

Q4

You are heading home near sunset and the tide has just turned against you! It's a pleasant evening for a Force 3 beat back up the estuary against the tide. You should:

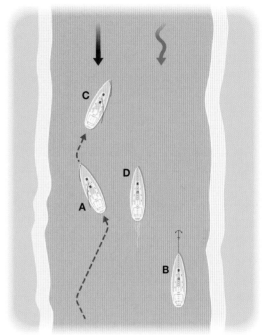

A Short tack close to the shoreline.

B Anchor and wait for the tide to turn.

C As A, but roll away some of the genoa.

D Motor up the center of the estuary so as to avoid the other yachts.

Answer: **B C**

Larger boats must be sailed through a tack, not thrown about. Any attempt to tack the boat quickly will cause the water flow around the rudder and keel to stall. By all means be positive with the wheel or tiller, but think "smooth," not "fast." Similarly, if you're lazy and leave the mainsheet pinned in tightly through the tack (easy with a sheet jammer), the airflow around the mainsail will stall, and you'll lose a couple of boat lengths to leeward before the flow is restored. The most effective approach is to ease the mainsheet by about 12–18 inches (30–45cm) as you luff for the tack, then pull it in again smoothly after the boat has borne away onto your new course.

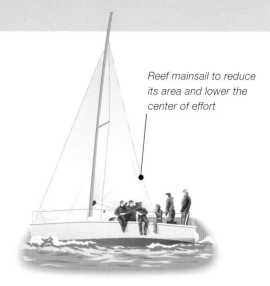

Reef mainsail to reduce its area and lower the center of effort

Classes vary, but it's usually quicker and more effective to reef the mainsail rather than change headsails.

Ease mainsail to allow for the change in apparent wind speed after the tack

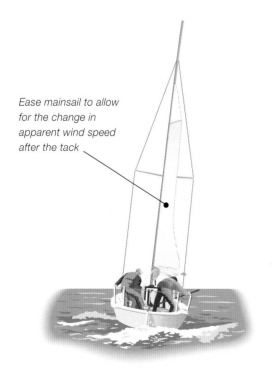

Answer: **A**

The majority of boats will handle better in these conditions under a reduced mainsail, rather than a smaller genoa. This is particularly true for boats with fractional rigs. Reefing will be quick and less work for the crew. It will also reduce the amount of weather helm caused by the boat heeling. A powerful genoa will help you through the waves if the wind veers, or initiate surfing if the wind backs.

All this is true for performance cruisers with a range of different headsails. If you're sailing a yacht with a roller-furling genoa, it's much more tempting just to take a few rolls in the genoa rather than reef the mainsail.

Answer: C

If you're sailing shorthanded, by far the easiest way to set off from a hove-to position is to bear away and jibe. That way, you're sailing again without having had to touch the sheets at all, let alone fight with flogging sheets in a rising wind. Going back a stage, if you're on passage in open water and want to heave to for any reason, the stress-free way to do it is to tack the boat without touching the genoa sheet. When you're ready to go again, the controlled jibe will get you back on your original course. The exception to this approach is when you're sailing in congested water. On these occasions you should heave to on starboard tack in order to give you right of way over most of the other sailboats you'll meet.

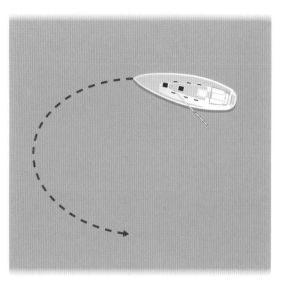

To get sailing again, simply pull the tiller to bear away and jibe.

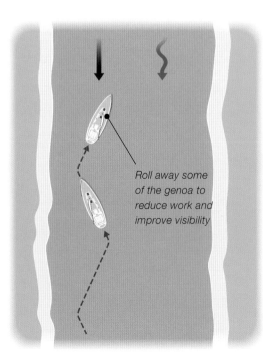

Roll away some of the genoa to reduce work and improve visibility

Answer: C

Assuming that you do decide to sail back, it's important to stay out of the strongest tide. By rolling away some of the genoa you might give away a little boat speed, but you'll increase visibility ahead and dramatically reduce the amount of work involved in tacking. Another more subtle consideration is that, with the tide against you, the apparent wind will be lower out in the center of the estuary where the tide is strongest, and this effect will be more marked as the tidal stream increases. Congratulations if you thought of that one!

Passage making

6.2

One of the great joys of cruising is that the whole sport moves up a gear from merely getting the best performance out of the rig. Wind, tide, weather, and route all play a part in your passage-making strategy. The reward is the experience of new places and people.

Q6 You're planning an offshore passage and estimate that it should take about 18 hours for you and your two crew. There's nothing but open sea between you and your destination—a small island with a safe harbor. None of you have visited the island, so you're excited about the trip. In this latitude, there are only 14 hours of daylight. You should:

A Set off four hours before dawn in order to reach your destination by sunset.

B Set off at nightfall in order to arrive in the middle of the following day.

C Set off in the early afternoon in order to arrive early the following morning.

Q5 In harbor, the night before a long passage, you're alongside the quay port side to. Just before you retire below, you should lock the mainsheet traveler:

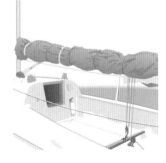

A On the centerline.

B To port.

C To starboard.

D It doesn't matter.

Q7 You're on an open-sea passage out of sight of land. Your destination is dead upwind, but you plan to be there by nightfall. The wind seems lighter than forecast, but the weather looks great, with lines of pure white cumulus marching across a fabulous blue sky. What's your strategy?

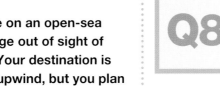

Q8 You're on passage from off-lying islands back toward the mainland, which is 5 miles (8km) off. Your destination is a harbor set in a featureless coastline. As the fog banks start to roll in, you curse the fact that you don't have any spare batteries for your GPS, and then plan a strategy. You should:

A Plot your current position, check the tides, and work out a course to steer that will take you to the harbor.

B Deliberately head off-course from your harbor destination and then turn for it when you're within sight of the coastline.

C Head back toward the safety of the islands while you can still see them.

D Stay well offshore until the fog lifts.

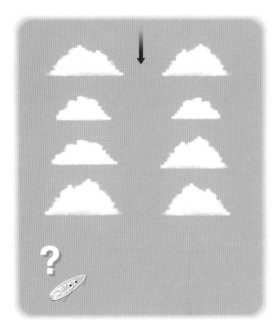

A Spend equal periods of time on each tack, noting the time as you tack.

B Sail on port tack until the wind increases.

C Stay within a 20-degree arc of your destination.

D Sail on starboard tack until you can lay the destination on port tack.

E Drop the sails and turn on the engine.

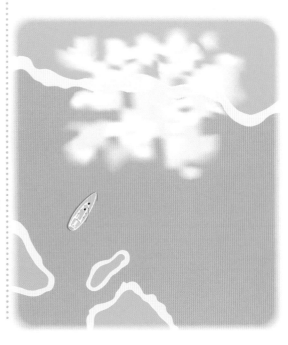

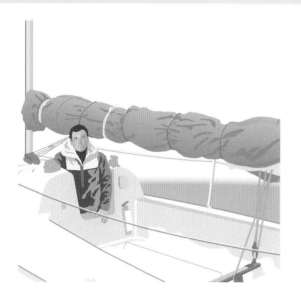

It's a simple way to avoid injury.

Answer: C

A5

The aim is to avoid a situation where one of the crew comes out on deck and bangs his or her head on the boom. The best solution is to position the boom on the side away from where people will be getting on and off the boat. As you're lying alongside to port in this example, the boom should be to starboard. It's always a useful routine to establish, but particularly important in a strange location, where you might find yourself having to come back on deck quickly—at night and disorientated.

Answer: C

A6

The two points to consider are the watch routine and the navigation. Option A will disturb everyone's sleep. Also, if you're slower than estimated, it means a night arrival in a strange place. Both B and C involve a night passage, but C has two advantages. You will be well into the passage by nightfall, so your watch-keeping routine will be established, and the crew is more likely to sleep. You will pick up the lights of the island toward the end of the night, confirming your position for the final approach.

Taking a landfall at dawn is a sure way to raise morale after a night at sea.

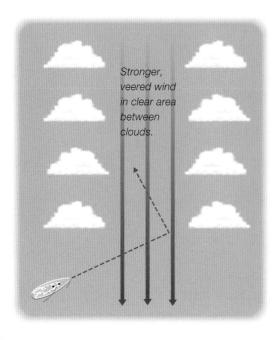

Stronger, veered wind in clear area between clouds.

Answer: B

The problem with the direct approach of A is that, if you don't arrive at the harbor mouth, you won't know which way to turn when you're within sight or soundings of the shore. In these conditions, the technique of "aiming-off" is the right approach. By heading 5 degrees upwind, you'll know that when you see the coastline or reach an appropriate depth of water you can turn, finding the harbor entrance about ½ mile (¾km) downwind. The other factor to remember is the principle of heading toward shallow water in poor visibility, so you're away from the danger of being run down by commercial shipping.

Answer: B

Even in stable conditions there are wind bands—areas of lighter and stronger winds. They're caused by "vortex rolls," where there's a vertical circulation of air moving up into the lines of cloud and down again into the clear areas between the clouds. Typically, these bands may be anything from 1 to 3 miles (2 to 5km) apart, with the stronger winds in the clear areas. So, if you're in the open sea and the wind is lighter than it should be, sail on port until you reach a strong wind band, then tack onto starboard to stay in it as long as possible.

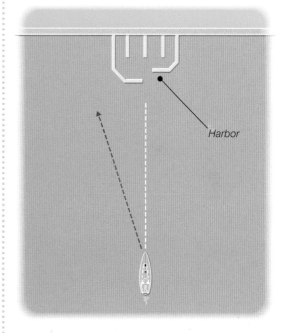

Harbor

Head upwind so the final approach will be easier.

6.3

Marina moments

Whether you are chartering or buying a yacht, learn how it handles in close quarters—both ahead and astern. This will give you confidence about getting the boat into and out of places you might have thought impossible. Choose a quiet spot away from other craft to practice.

Q9 You've chartered a cruising sailboat, which is lying alongside the jetty, ready for you to set off. What's the best way to find out which way the stern will swing when the engine goes astern?

A Take the boat out and see how tightly she turns to port and to starboard.

B With the boat still alongside, put the engine in gear, take off the engine cover, and see which way the prop shaft turns.

C With the boat still alongside, put the engine in gear ahead, and see which way the bow swings.

D With the boat still alongside, put the engine in gear astern, and look over both sides of the boat near the stern.

Q10 The wind has changed direction and increased during the evening while you've been alongside the jetty. Although it was on the beam, it's now blowing straight down the hatch, and you want to turn the boat around before nightfall for a quieter night. The best way to do this is to:

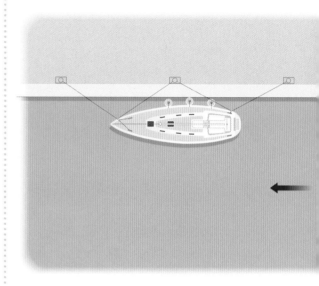

A Motor out stern first, turn through 180 degrees, and then reverse back alongside.

B Rig a long rope from the bow outside everything, cast off the bow line, and pull the boat around head to wind, keeping the stern to the jetty.

C Rig a long rope from the stern outside everything and cast off the stern line to pull the boat head to wind, with the bow to the jetty.

The boat is secured properly, with bow and stern lines, and two spring lines. She's lying head to wind alongside the jetty, and you're ready to go. With only two of you on board, in which order should you untie the warps?

A Take off both spring lines and then the stern line, leaving the bow line until last.

B Take off the bow line, the stern line, and then the stern spring line, leaving the bow spring line until last.

C Rig the stern spring line as a slip line, take off the bow spring line and stern line, and then the bow line.

D Rig the stern line as a slip line, take off the bow line and both spring lines, and leave the stern line until last.

You enter a crowded yacht marina, where the only berth is in a tight spot up a dead-end alley. The stern of your boat kicks strongly to port when the engine starts going astern. Your best way to approach the berth is to:

A Motor slowly past the berth, turn to starboard, and then reverse in to port.

B Swing wide to starboard as you approach, drifting in so you don't need the engine.

C Overcompensate with the approach, so your final touch of astern power straightens up the boat.

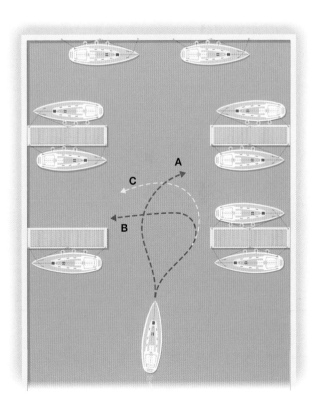

Answer: D

A9 Most cruising boats enjoy what's known as "prop wash" or "paddle-wheel effect," especially those with inboard engines and fixed three-bladed propellers. Almost unnoticeable when the boat is moving ahead, this effect causes the stern to swing one way or the other when the engine's running astern, especially if the boat is moving very slowly. By looking over each side of the boat near the stern, you should see the water flow created by the propeller. If the wash is coming out to starboard, it means that the stern will kick to port when going astern, and vice versa.

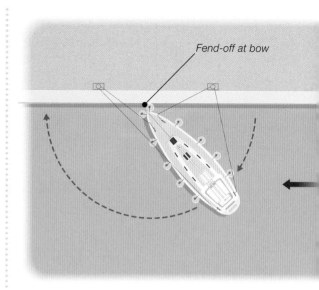

Fend-off at bow

With a fend-off at the bow and more on both sides, this should be a very simple maneuver.

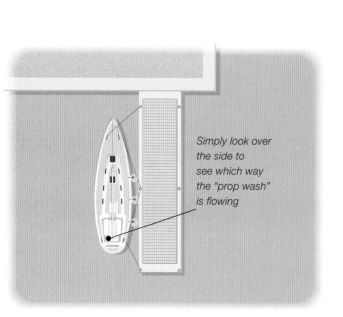

Simply look over the side to see which way the "prop wash" is flowing

It's important to know which way the stern will swing before you set off.

Answer: C

A10 Close call, this one, as in principle there's no reason why B shouldn't work either. On the majority of boats, however, there are two factors that make C more effective. The first is that, with the typical tendency for the bow to pay off downwind, the first half of your warping maneuver is going to be hard work if you go for B. The second is that there tends to be less clutter at the bow, and the hull shape makes it easier to avoid damage.

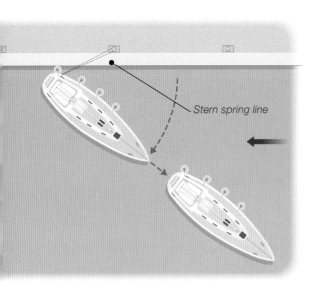

Double the stern spring so that it can be slipped from aboard the boat.

 **Answer: C**

Your aim is to let the bow swing away from the jetty without letting the boat drop astern. It's a good move to put a fend-off at the point on the stern where you judge the boat might touch the jetty. The bow line and stern spring line will hold the boat securely while you tidy away the other ropes and prepare to depart. It is likely that when you let go the bow line, the bow will drift out of its own accord. This is because most yachts have a tendency for the bow to pay off downwind. If not, a touch of astern power against the stern spring line will nudge the bow out. If you're leaving under sail, you'll need to back the headsail to encourage the bow to pay off on the tack that takes you away from the jetty.

 **Answer: A**

Not only does this approach give you the most control, it also sets you up for the simplest departure. You'll have to judge how much astern power you need to get the swing right, before you ease back into neutral to slip into the space. Finish up with a touch of power ahead to stop the boat. The final advantage of this approach is that, if it does go wrong, you've completed half the turn you need for a dignified exit from the alley.

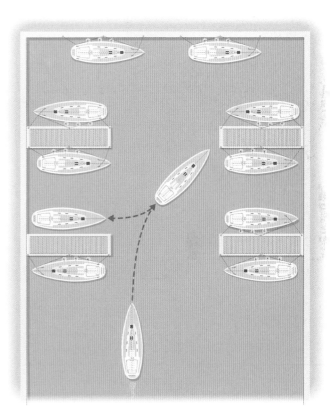

Prepare for close quarters' handling like this by checking out your boat's swinging circle and stopping distance in safe, open water.

6.4

Anchoring and mooring

Before you do anything, take a few moments to analyze the conditions. What are wind and tide doing now, and what will they be doing in a few hours? Which way will the boat lie when you stop? Now plan your approach and brief the crew.

Q13

You're planning a lunch stop in a tidal estuary, and you've identified a suitable spot. If you approach on a broad reach into the tide, what's the best way to anchor under sail?

A Roll away the genoa and approach under mainsail alone.

B Sail beyond your planned spot and head up into the wind.

C Luff first, lower the mainsail, and approach downwind under genoa alone.

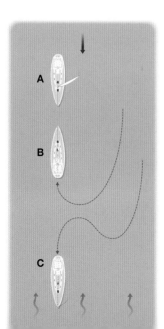

Q14

It's a perfect night to anchor in a stunning location, but the bay is crowded. The wind is blowing a shifting Force 3. Your lightweight cruiser carries 2 yards (2m) of chain, and the rest of the anchor warp is nylon. The only sensible spot is among some much larger yachts, both power and sail, where the depth is 30 feet (9m). What's your strategy?

A Pick a friendly-looking crew and ask if you can moor alongside them for the night.

B Choose the center of the available spot to drop anchor, and since you're using rope, lay out 50 yards (45m) of anchor warp.

C Lay your anchor toward the upwind side of the space, lay out 30 yards (27m) of warp, and chuck a bucket out on a line astern.

D Forget this anchorage and head back out to sea for the night.

Q15

It's a vile afternoon for a passage. It's blowing SW Force 5–6 and it's been raining for hours. Ahead, there's an island with a couple of anchorages and a small harbor. You decide to stop to let the weather blow through. Your best option is:

A The anchorage on the NW side of the island.

B The anchorage on the SE side of the island.

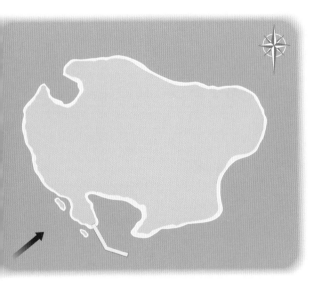

C The small harbor on the SW side of the island.

Q16

After an overnight stop, you're up early to catch the tide. There's virtually no wind, but the tide has started to ebb. You go on deck to find that two other yachts have arrived quietly during the night and are moored outside your boat. You should:

A Wake their crews and tell them you're leaving.

B Go back to bed until they wake up.

C Rearrange their warps and head off downtide.

D Rearrange their warps and head off into the tide.

E Cast them off and head out quietly.

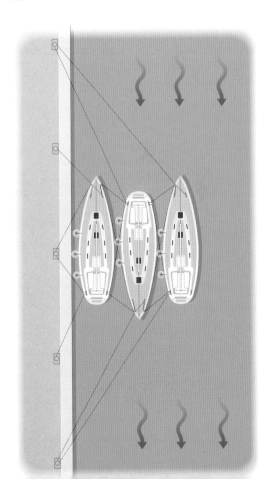

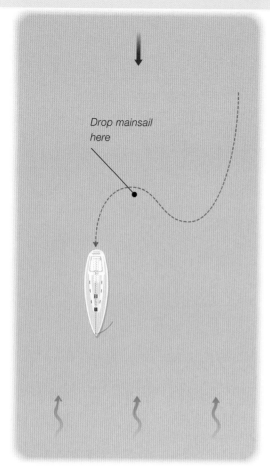

Drop mainsail here

Answer: **C**

Although the usual rule of thumb for anchoring is 3x depth for chain and 5x depth for rope, you can lie to much less in very settled conditions. The problem with laying out too much warp is that you're likely to swing all over the anchorage in the shifting wind, probably bumping into other boats. A bucket hanging on a short length of line does a fine job of damping your boat's movement. In these conditions, the wind is likely to drop right away at night, but it's still worth setting an alarm for the early hours, just to check that everything's OK. If you're really bold, or know someone in one of the large boats, Answer A is an option, providing that you lay out your anchor, rather than relying solely on theirs. You must also ensure that the boats are moored so that the masts aren't in line.

Lay your anchor close astern of the boat to windward.

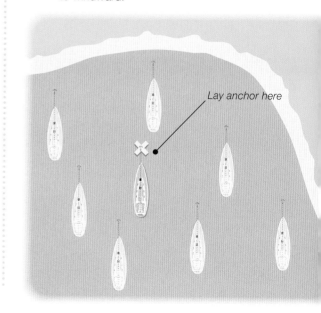

Lay anchor here

Answer: **C**

When you anchor in a tidal stream, the boat will end up headed into the tide, so you've got to get the mainsail down first. The rest's a dream because you can use the genoa as both accelerator and brake to control your speed of approach. In a strong wind, you may have to roll most of it away before you anchor. Getting away is equally easy—leave under genoa and luff to hoist the mainsail when you're in clear water. Of course, if the tide has turned while you've been having lunch, your departure will be under mainsail and genoa.

A15

Answer: B

You're in the middle of a frontal depression, a classic weather system. Forget the harbor. You'd be approaching a lee shore in poor conditions, and even if there's room for you, the swell would make for a very uncomfortable night. Once the cold front passes through, the wind will veer to the NW and become gusty, making the anchorage on that side of the island untenable.

Note: If you're sailing in the Southern Hemisphere, the correct answer is A. The SW wind suggests that it's already veered and that the rain will soon stop. Any further change in wind direction is likely to be further south.

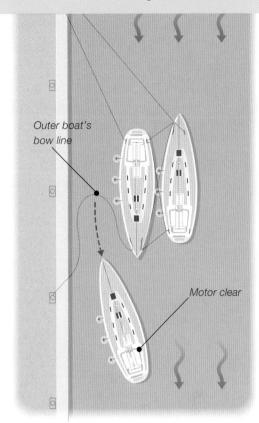

Outer boat's bow line

Motor clear

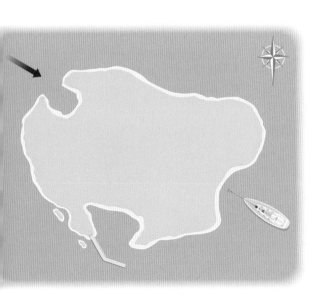

In these conditions, plan for what the weather will be doing in a few hours time.

A16

Answer: C

This is the exception to the normal principle of leaving a berth into the tide. Of more concern is that you don't disturb the warps that are keeping the other boats in position. Your first step is to recover your own bow and stern lines. Next, untie the downtide shore lines from the boats outside you. Re-lead them all the way around your boat and back to the shore. Unfasten the lines from your boat and slip out downtide. You'll need to leave one of your crew on the other boats to secure their lines properly. Pick him or her up from the outside boat when the job's done. You can judge the maneuver a success if you complete the whole thing without waking a soul!

Racing Skills

7

Although many who start their sailing in cabin boats never become involved in racing, those who sail smaller boats can be winning club races during their first season. The challenge of competition and the social life that goes with it holds many people in a single class for years.

Luckily, sailing is one sport where you're not condemned to be a veteran by the age of 30, and where experience and sly cunning are often more than a match for strength and youthful agility.

The racing rules have been greatly simplified in recent years, and most of this section applies whether you're racing a single-handed dinghy, beach catamaran, or lager cabin yacht.

7.1

The **start**

It's often said that getting a good start accounts for 90 percent of winning. Whether you're sailing a single-hander, or a fully crewed offshore yacht, all the questions in this section apply. How good are you on the line?

Q1

You've heard that all the best sailboat racers get out to the course well before the start, in order to check out the wind. What exactly are they looking for?

A Patterns in the timing of gusts and lulls.

B Shifts in wind direction.

C Whether the rig is properly set up.

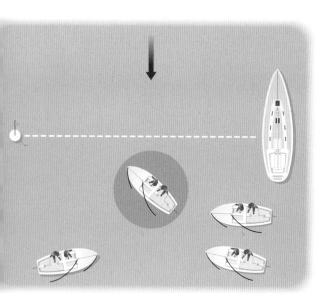

Q2

You're out at the start line early, trying to assess which is the favored end. Without a compass in the boat, you can do this by:

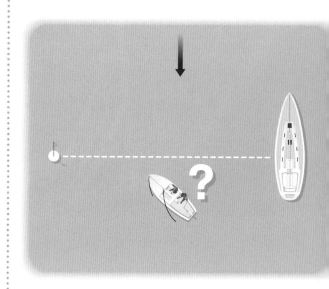

A Seeing which end is favored by the top helmsmen in the fleet.

B Going head-to-wind at the middle of the line, and seeing which end of the line appears closer to the bow.

C Asking the people on the committee boat.

D Sailing up the line one way, then the other, noting how much mainsheet tension is required to keep the sail full.

Q3 You're part of a big club fleet of one-design sailboats, and lucky enough to have a Race Officer who usually sets start lines with very little bias. You've noticed that the people who start at the ends of the line consistently end up in the leading group at the windward mark. This is because:

A They're the best sailors.

B It's easier to judge the start from close to the ends.

C The fleet creates its own wind bend.

D They're staying away from the crowd in the middle of the line.

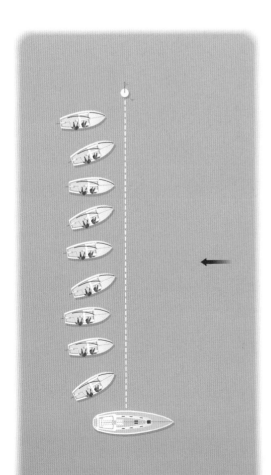

 Q4 In spite of your best efforts, you find yourself to leeward of a group of one-design boats, with all of you crossing the line on starboard tack. The best thing now is probably to:

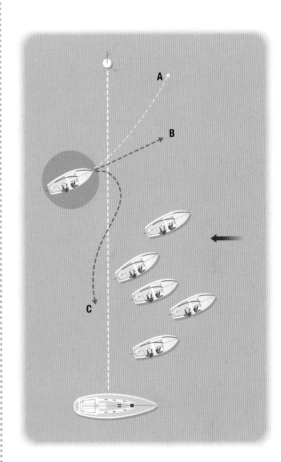

A Ease sheets and bear away.

B Stay put, and concentrate on sailing the boat as flat and fast as possible.

C Tack onto port as soon as possible.

111

Answer: A B

In many areas, there are regular patterns to the variations in wind speed and direction in certain weather conditions. By getting out to the start line early, you can note the patterns before the race and take advantage of them. For example, a wind shift ten minutes before the start might encourage newcomers to favor one end of the line, whereas those who have been monitoring the shifts know that the wind will shift back again after about seven to eight minutes. Even if they notice the shift, the newcomers will find it impossible to get back to the right end.

Take a waterproof pen or pencil and write the timings and direction of gusts and windshifts directly on the boat.

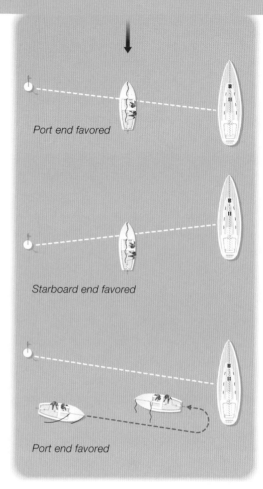

Port end favored

Starboard end favored

Port end favored

Answer: B D

On a short line, it's often possible to check the bias simply by going head-to-wind in the middle of the line. The end of the line that is more to windward is the favored end. On a longer line, with plenty of boats around, it is difficult to do this. Instead, sail up the line one way, tack or jibe around, and sail along the line the other way. If you have had to sheet in to maintain the right sheet tension on the second reach, you're sailing toward the favored end of the line. If you've had to sheet out, you're sailing away from the favored end.

Answer: B C

In a large fleet it's very difficult to judge your start when you're at the middle of the line, because other boats may prevent you from seeing the ends. For this reason, in some big fleet starts, an extra buoy is positioned in the middle of the line. A large fleet creates a wall of sails, so think how the wind will have to bend to get around the edges of that wall. This bend will favor starboard tackers at the port end of the line, and vice versa. This is why it's a common, and winning, big-fleet tactic to start at the starboard end of the line and tack straight onto port. You take advantage of the wind bend, and are then in a commanding tactical position for the first beat.

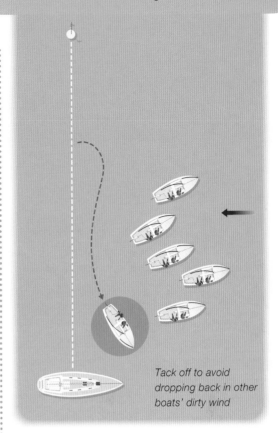

Tack off to avoid dropping back in other boats' dirty wind

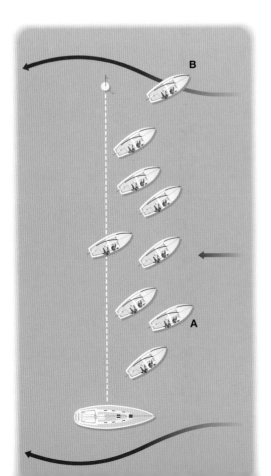

Answer: C

In most one-design fleets, there's not a great deal of difference in boat speed upwind, so the best course of action will be to tack away into clear wind as soon as you possibly can. Before you go, look out for other boats to windward and astern, because you'll have to give way to them as you cross the remainder of the fleet. If there's no room to tack clear, ease the sheets very slightly, and head for clear air to leeward, accepting that your extra speed won't make up for the ground you lose.

Boats A and B have the best starts, but A is favored by being on the starboard side.

7.2

The **windward** legs

In non-planing fleets and/or light weather conditions, the windward legs see plenty of place changes, because some racers make huge gains by using wind shifts effectively.

Q5 You are racing on a large lake in shifting wind conditions. The windward leg is about a mile (2km) long. You have the choice of heading out toward the shore on either side, or tacking up the middle of the course. You should:

A Take a long tack toward the starboard side of the course.

B Watch the others and then go with the majority of the fleet.

C Tack each time you are headed, aiming to stay near the middle of the course.

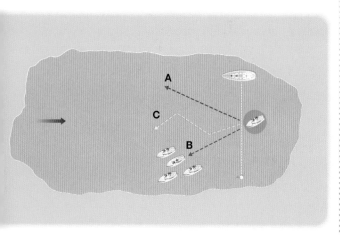

Q6 You're sailing close-hauled on port tack, approaching a boat on starboard. At this stage, you're not sure whether you can cross safely ahead of the other boat. You should:

A Stand on for a while, until you know for sure whether you can cross ahead.

B Crack sheets for speed, accepting that you'll have to duck its stern.

C Tack now.

Q7 You're racing in a one-design fleet, sailing on starboard, and a port-tacker has just tacked immediately under your port bow, so that it's ahead and to leeward. You should:

 Q8 You're approaching the windward mark on port tack, only to find a long procession of boats coming in on the starboard layline. The mark is still about 20 boat lengths away. Your best tactic is:

A Stand on to sail right over the other boat.

A To sail as high as you can and hope for a gap when you need to tack around the mark.

B To sail fast and free, looking for a gap where you can sneak between two of the approaching boats, and then tack onto starboard.

C To maintain your best upwind course, aiming to tack when you hit the layline, and dealing with any boats you meet at the appropriate time.

B Bear away until you hit the other boat to prove that it's in the wrong.

C Tack away onto port now.

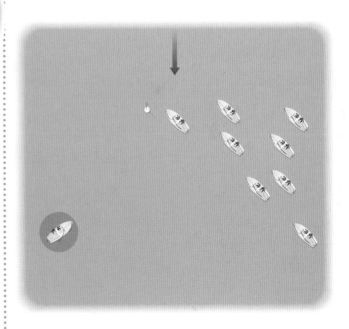

115

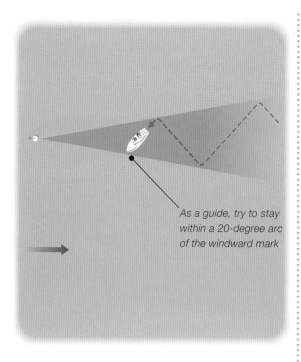

As a guide, try to stay within a 20-degree arc of the windward mark

Answer: A

A6 There's no point in making a decision that is going to cost you places until you have to. Stand on, aiming for maximum speed, and keeping an eye on the other boat. As you get closer, it will become clear whether you can cross its bow safely; tack onto starboard just before the other boat to lee bow it, or ease sheets and duck under its stern. Considerations that will affect your choice include the proximity of other boats, and whether you want to be over on the starboard side of the course yet, preparing to hit the layline for the windward mark.

Don't be rushed into an early decision, but let the starboard tacker know that you've seen him.

Answer: C

A5 In a wind that shifts regularly, you should always tack when you are headed and avoid getting too far to one side of the course or the other. If you stay near the middle, you can gain ground on each wind shift, whereas if you go out to one of the corners, your ability to take advantage of wind shifts will be restricted by your need to stay on the layline for the windward mark. The only exception would be if there was a known advantage in one shore or the other. Large lakes can be affected by wind bends, which usually favor the port side of the course in the Northern Hemisphere (starboard side in the Southern Hemisphere).

Tack clear, then back onto starboard on the next shift

Answer: C

A7

Difficult call, this one, but assuming that the other boat has tacked efficiently and you believe it'll have the same boat speed as you, it's unlikely that you'll be able to drive over the top of it to windward. The lee-bow effect is so strong that the dirty wind pushed up from its sails will affect your pointing and boat speed. By tacking away onto port, you'll be in clear air and can concentrate on getting maximum boat speed before you meet again in a couple of tacks' time.

Answer: C

A8

Because of its nightmare potential, many helmsmen take the safe option and get onto the starboard layline early. That, in turn, increases the scope for the brave and the bold, who rely on the fact that many of those coming in on starboard will have overstood the mark, making room for the port-tacker, who can sneak in, tack, and lee-bow someone. The leading boats that have already rounded will provide a wind shadow as you approach, although they'll also bend the apparent wind in your favor. Finally, don't forget that, if you tack for the mark inside the two-boat-length zone, you must keep clear of other boats until you are close-hauled, and you must also give room to any starboard-tacker that gains an overlap.

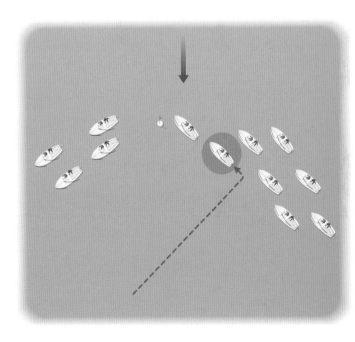

In a big fleet, there's almost always room for you to join the boats on the layline.

7.3 The **offwind** legs

In non-planing boats and light winds, the offwind legs can be processional, but in faster boats and stronger winds they provide scope for massive differences in speed, depending on how well each helmsman masters the conditions. How would you fare?

You've rounded the windward mark in third place, close astern of a pair of boats that are now reaching on the layline to the jibe mark and hoisting their spinnakers. You should:

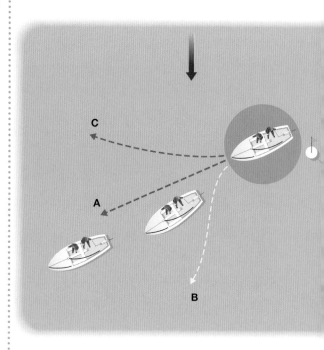

A Stay on the layline and hoist your spinnaker.

B Hoist your spinnaker and go low to avoid their dirty wind.

C Go high, delaying your spinnaker hoist.

After a brilliant start and clear wind all the way up the beat, you round the windward mark in first place. The next leg is a reach, but too fine to hoist the spinnaker at this stage. With other boats close behind, your tactic should be:

A To stick to the rhumb line.

B To sail high first.

C To get the spinnaker up quickly and sail low, rounding up later.

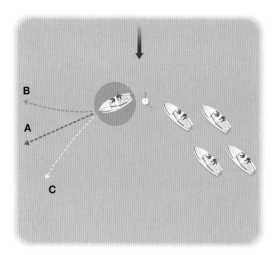

Q11 You're racing in a handicap fleet, sailing down a reach with a boat of the same class about three boat lengths to windward, and just astern of you. You glance back to see another larger boat approaching, and it looks as if it's going to try to sail through the gap between you. You should:

A Luff hard now to make it clear that there is no gap.

B Luff slowly, warning the larger boat of your intention.

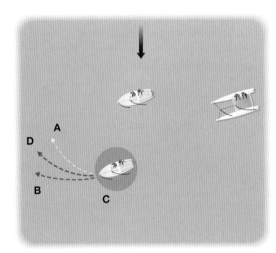

C Do nothing—at that speed it'll soon be past you.

D Wait until the larger boat has an overlap, and then luff hard.

Q12 You are approaching the leeward mark on port. Another group of boats is ahead of you and approaching the mark on starboard. As you reach the two-boat-length zone, you realize that you have no overlap. The mark is to be rounded to port. You should:

A Take your medicine and go outside the boats, giving them the room they need. After all, you can make up for it on the next beat.

B Try to sail as close as possible to leeward of the boats, forcing them to jibe quickly as they round, and hence slow down.

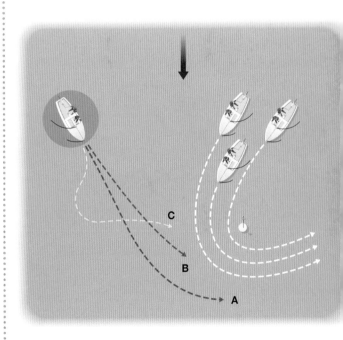

C Slow down yourself.

Answer: B

By sailing high, you are establishing a defensive position against the boats behind you and dissuading them from trying to sail over you to windward. You're also better placed to take advantage of any wind shift, whether it backs or veers. When the boats behind start to drop to leeward, you must too. In this way, they'll have no chance of establishing an overlap before the next mark. If you've kept the same advantage on this leg as you did on the first, you'll also be in the best position to hoist the spinnaker first when your course, or a veering wind shift, allows.

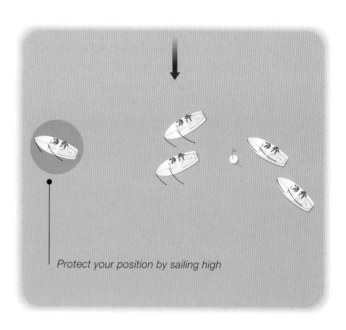

Protect your position by sailing high

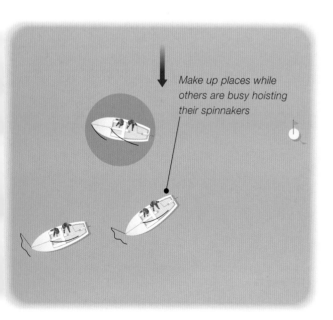

Make up places while others are busy hoisting their spinnakers

Answer: C

If you drop in behind the other boats, that's exactly where you'll stay. Similarly, if you aim to go low, the chances are that you'll still be affected by their dirty wind. As long as you are close astern, you stand a good chance of sailing over the other boats while they're concentrating on hoisting their spinnakers. Assuming that you've practiced the drills and get a smooth, quick spinnaker hoist, you'll find that the other boats will have to suffer your dirty wind.

Answer: **B**

You have to accept that the larger boat will pass you; the important thing is to encourage it to sail to leeward. If you luff hard, you risk putting yourself into the wind shadow of the small boat, which could lead to a luffing match costing you both places. If you do nothing, your loss of speed when the large boat sails over you will also allow the other small boat to pass you, costing you a place. As long as both other boats are clear astern, you are perfectly in your rights to luff and protect your wind. Leave it too late, and you risk a serious situation if the other boat doesn't respond in time.

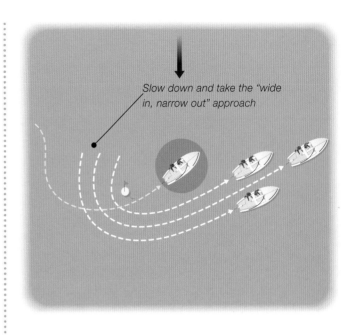

Slow down and take the "wide in, narrow out" approach

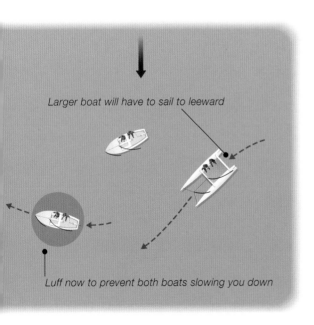

Larger boat will have to sail to leeward

Luff now to prevent both boats slowing you down

Answer: **C**

This is a real case of "slow down to win." If you haven't established an overlap outside the two-boat-length zone, you have no right to room at the mark. The inside boats coming in on starboard will have to jibe quickly in order to stay clear of the boats overlapped outside them, and it's highly likely that they'll leave a gap close to the mark. If you slow down by sheeting the mainsail in tightly (and lowering the plate in a centerboarder), you'll be able to line up for a smooth, tight rounding close to the mark. You may not pass the whole group, but the chances are that you'll make up several places.

121

The final **beat**

7.4

The previous windward legs will have set a pattern for the final beat. Unless conditions have changed, you should know whether to go left, or right, or play the shifts up the middle. You'll also know by now whether you're still attacking boats in front, or defending your place against those astern.

Q13 **It's the last leg of the race and you're in front. As you round the leeward mark, you're 200 yards (180m) ahead and the only thing between you and the finish line is a one-mile (2km) beat. Earlier, the starboard side of the beat was favored. You should:**

A Head for the starboard side and concentrate on your own boat speed.

B Go right, and tack when the next boat rounds the leeward mark.

C Go right and tack when the next boat is still 100 yards (90m) from the leeward mark.

Q14 **As you approach the finishing line, it looks as if port tack is favored, so which end of the finishing line should you aim for?**

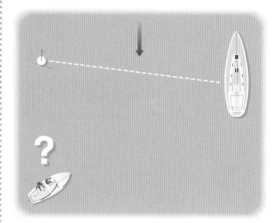

A The starboard end.

B The port end.

C The opposite end to where you started.

7.5 Racing bigger boats **offshore**

You may think that you're a pretty good sailboat racer, but as soon as you enter the world of offshore racing, you start learning all over again. There's so much more to consider. To give you a taste, see how you'd rate with the big boys' toys.

Starting from a long line, the first leg is a reach on starboard to a turning mark offshore. The wind is Force 2. The current is setting across your course from the port side. The favored end of the start line is:

A The windward end.

B The leeward end.

C It doesn't matter, as there's no beat involved.

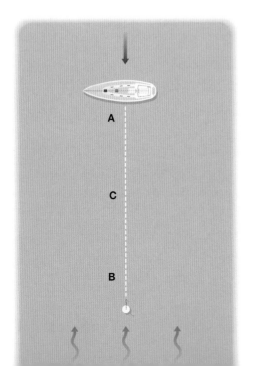

Because of your racing experience in small sailboats, you've been invited aboard a cruiser for an early-season, offshore-passage race along the coast. The crew is smart, but they're looking to you for racing knowledge. The light gradient wind is almost astern, so you're enjoying a broad spinnaker reach with the coastline about a mile (2km) off your starboard beam. During the afternoon, there's been more wind at this distance from the coast and you've made up ground on those who stayed well offshore. Assuming that the tide isn't a factor in the decision, your strategy as dusk approaches should be to:

A Head offshore.

B Stay where you are.

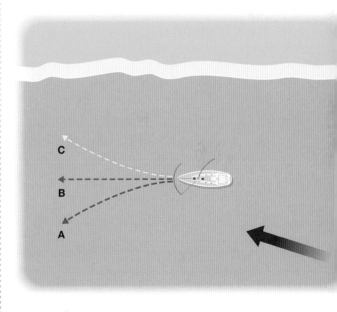

C Head further inshore.

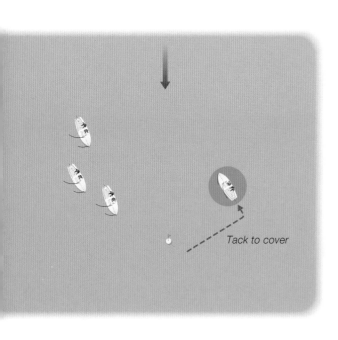

Tack to cover

Answer: C

A13 The principle here is to keep directly between the opposition and the finish line. By tacking when the next boat has halved the distance to the mark, you'll be directly upwind of it as it rounds the leeward mark. You can then stay in control, regardless of which way it goes and whether the wind shifts to left or right.

Note how much lead you have when rounding the mark, and tack when the next boat is about half that distance from the mark.

Answer: A

A14 The favored tack for the final beat is the one that takes you across the finishing line closest to 90 degrees. The simple rule to remember is that the favored end is opposite to the favored tack (if the favored tack is port, the favored end is starboard). In clubs where the start line is used to finish, this rule is only true if the line has not been altered and the wind hasn't shifted.

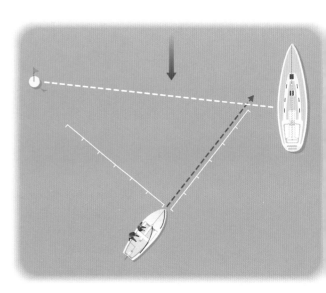

As a final check, when you cross the layline to the other end, you can confirm that your favored end is nearer.

Answer: B

In a reaching start across the tide or current, it always pays to start uptide. In the diagram, boat A with the upwind start will have to bear away and stem the tide to reach the mark, whereas the uptide boat B will enjoy increased apparent wind as the tide pushes it toward the mark. The longer the start line relative to the leg length, the greater the effect will be.

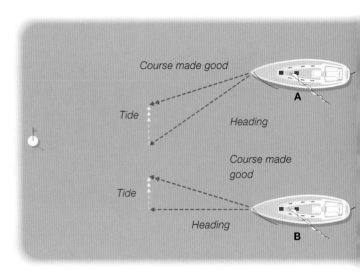

Answer: B

Below a height of about 1,500 feet (450m), the true gradient wind is affected by surface drag, which causes the wind to back. The amount of this drag varies, according to whether the wind is blowing over the land or the sea. Where the two meet, there's a zone of convergence or divergence, depending on the wind direction relative to the shore. In this example, the wind direction indicates that the stronger wind a mile (2km) offshore has nothing to do with a sea breeze effect. Although diurnal effects are likely to make the wind speed drop overnight, the "coastal freeway" effect is likely to stay. Get this right and your cruising friends will be well impressed.

Note: The effect is reversed if the coastline is on your left, because of wind divergence.

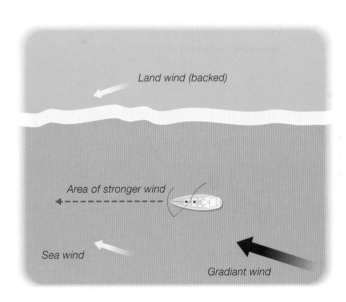

Glossary and **Index**

Backstay A wire from the mast to the stern of the boat, providing fore-and-aft support

Beam The side of the boat

Bearing away Turning away from the wind

Beat A course to windward, involving at least one tack

Camber The lateral shape of a sail

Clew The lower aft corner of a sail

Close-hauled Sailing as close to the wind as possible

Cunningham A rope that controls tension and hence the shape of the leading edge of a sail

Feathering Allowing the leading edge of a sail to flap slightly

Forestay A wire supporting the mast

Genoa A large, overlapping jib

GPS Global Positioning System

Guy A rope or wire supporting the tack of a spinnaker

Heeling The lateral angle of a boat from vertical

Jibing Turning the boat so that its stern passes through the wind

Kiting Heeling the boat deliberately to windward

Layline The direct line to a windward mark (without tacking)

Leech The back edge of a sail

Leeward Side away from the wind

Luff 1. The leading edge of a sail
2. To turn towards the wind

Planing Increasing speed by riding on the boat's own bow wave

Rhumb line The shortest route point to point

Sheet The rope attached to the clew of a sail, controlling its position and power

Shroud A wire supporting the mast laterally

Skeg A fin on the underside of the boat, contributing to directional stability

Spring lines Mooring warps that control the fore-and-aft surge of the boat

Tack 1. The lower front corner of the sail
2. To turn the boat so that its bow passes through the wind

Vang A rope or wire that limits boom lift and sail twist

Quarto and the author gratefully acknowledge the enthusiastic help of Alan Williams and his staff at Plas Menai, the Welsh National Watersports Centre, in modeling the action sequences throughout this book.

Quarto would like to acknowledge and thank the following for supplying pictures reproduced in this book:

p. 2 John Driscoll
p. 5 Ian Howes
p. 8 Sports Council for Wales
p. 9 Sports Council for Wales
p. 16 Ian Howes
p. 22 Sports Council for Wales
p. 23 Sports Council for Wales
p. 44 Sports Council for Wales
p. 45 Sports Council for Wales
p. 47 Ian Howes
p. 49 Ian Howes
p. 54 Ian Howes
p. 55 Ian Howes
p. 72 Ian Howes
p. 73 Ian Howes
p. 75 Ian Howes
p. 78 Ian Howes
p. 86 Ian Howes
p. 90 Sports Council for Wales
p. 91 Sports Council for Wales
p. 93 John Driscoll
p. 96 Sports Council for Wales
p. 98 Ian Howes
p. 100 Ian Howes
p. 108 Sports Council for Wales
p. 109 Sports Council for Wales
p. 112 John Driscoll
p. 122 John Driscoll